Why Do You Cry?

Why Do You Cry?

Lori L. Edwards

iUniverse, Inc.
New York   Bloomington

Why Do You Cry?

iUniverse books may be ordered through booksellers or by contacting:

iUniverse

1663 Liberty Drive

Bloomington, IN 47403

www.iuniverse.com

1-800-Authors (1-800-288-4677)

Because of the dynamic nature of the Internet, any Web addresses or links contained in this book may have changed since publication and may no longer be valid. The views expressed in this work are solely those of the author and do not necessarily reflect the views of the publisher, and the publisher hereby disclaims any responsibility for them.

ISBN: 978-1-4401-9954-7 (pbk)

ISBN: 978-1-4401-9953-0 (ebk)

Printed in the United States of America

iUniverse rev. date: 12/03/09

Introduction

"For I know the plans I have for you," declared the Lord, *"plans to prosper you, not to harm you, but to give you an expected end."* Jeremiah 29:11-13

If I had a dime for every time I have seen that scripture on a billboard or a T-shirt, I would probably be a rich woman. However, like many other single woman in the world, I often wondered, "When, God? When do my plans start? God, please tell me why do I have to cry so many tears."

Let me take you back on a seven-year's journey with me as I search for the answer to this dilemma, a journey filled with ups and downs and spiritual revelations of how God does work things out for the good in our lives. I pray that you will enjoy this journey with me as you chuckle at the mistakes I make along the way. In the end, you may discover that, contrary to your original thoughts, we have a lot in common when it comes to the way God deals with us.

Nowadays, many people keep a journal, and I am one of them. In the beginning, I felt as if God was urging me to keep a record of my journey, but I did not understand why. Nevertheless, as time went by, I began to understand the purpose of my pain and my tears through writing my journals. No, I did not always want to share my personal thoughts, but I reluctantly submitted to the Father's will, and now I understand why I had to cry so many tears. I cry for my daughters, Loren and Ashley. I cry for my brothers Evan and Bill. I cry for my sisters Shari, Marla, Stephanie, and Tina, and for my best girls Chaneasha, Yolanda, Alisha, and Shannon. I cry for Mom, Dad, and my Step Dad Vern who has been such a blessing to me. I cry for those who have not yet felt the great storms of life. I cry for those who are presently in a storm. I cry for anyone whose heart has ever been shattered into a millions pieces. And, most of all, I cried for the love of God to fill my heart with peace and restoration, so that I can help others to realize that God can and will, absolutely and completely, heal their broken hearts.

I need you to bear with me through part one It seems that I was stuck on stupid longer than one should be. However, for those who are going through a painful divorce: I pray that part one will be of assistance and encouragement, that no matter how bad it hurts,   God will not leave you there. This is part of the process of healing.

PART ONE: "KATRINA"

Chapter One

It is funny how we can be warned that a storm is coming, but, for some reason, we think it could hit everyone else's house except ours. In early 2002, winds were blowing 50 mile per hour; trees were even swaying back and forth. Violent waves were crashing against the coastline of my life; yet, in spite of all the warning signs, I had not seen the storm coming. Like Hurricane Katrina, a major storm called Divorce disrupted my life. Did I deserve it? First, ask my family; then, ask "his." This was called "the blame game." It didn't do much good down South, and it probably wasn't going to help here either. All that I knew was that at thirty-five years old, I was left alone to raise two little girls, ages ten and twelve. The damage had been done, and now it was time to clean up the mess the storm had left behind!

April 15, 2002

Dear God, I give you the honor, glory, and praise. My husband has been gone for one month now. I can't breathe without him. I feel as though I want to die. If it were not for my kids and the fact that suicide is murder in your eyes, I would be planning my own death. I have bargained with you for the last forty-five days. Where are you? Can a sister get an answer?

Two days later, I received my divorce papers in the mail. I felt as David did in II Samuel after he had begged God to spare the child that he and Bathsheba had conceived in sin. After David was told his son was dead, he got up, dried his eyes, and ate. For the rest of that day, I didn't cry. Yes, my hope for reconciliation was gone, but I now had a new plan. Maybe God would put us back together again after the divorce. I figured that if I was really good and I tried really hard, He would grant my request. After all, "God specializes in things that are impossible." As I previously said, I still had a plan, but, then, so did God.

During this time in my life, I met a woman who considered herself a "prophet of God." She wanted to be called "Prophetess," so that is what I called her. I would visit with her three to four times a week, and she would personally minister to me. She spoke of my past and of the future that she felt God had for me. Because I was so desperate for answers from God, I ate up everything she said like a saint who had just come off a forty-day fast. When our sessions became too painful for me, emotionally – I would do what most people did when they were in painful situations. I ran, not from her – although that did not seem like a bad idea either– but from God.

During this time, I was still operating The White House Coffee Shop located on Grissom Air Force Base near Peru, IN.

The shop was a joint effort between my husband, Mom, my sister Stephanie, and me. After my husband left, my mother, who was my rock, and Stephanie, who was my beautiful hostess, still worked with me. Initially, the business was very successful partly due to my husband's popularity with the customers. Many military men who enjoyed coming into my coffee shop for my good coffee also liked to admire my sister's beauty.

While my husband Shawn was working at the shop, I was using my income from my job at Chrysler to keep the coffee shop going, but when he left, he took half of our income with him. Thanks to Mom and Stephanie, who continued to help me, and in spite of the fact that I was short of help, the shop continued to be a success. However, now that Shawn was gone, I had to face all the household responsibilities as well as those of The White House...alone! A shattered mind, in addition to pain of the divorce, and having to run the shop without Shawn's support finally overwhelmed me. In July 2002, four months after my husband had left, the doors of The White House Coffee closed.

My marriage was now gone! My business had failed! My life was in disarray! What was next? It was a cruel, cruel summer!

Chapter Two

Now that I had officially hit rock bottom, it was time to call on God. What? Did you ask me why I hadn't called on Him sooner? Well, actually, I had, but I did not like the way He had answered me. He...of all people...wanted me to submit! Submit to what? After all that I had been through this past summer, the last thing I wanted to do was submit. But I had no peace. How could I find peace? I thought maybe I would date around, you know, just as friends: That was how I spent my summer. However...I still had no peace! I was hormonal, insecure, and desperate, not to mention miserable.

"O.K., God, we will try it your way," I finally agreed.

Why did I refer to myself as "we"? Well, I admit I had some friends I carried along with me. Let's see, there was Depression as well as my friend Defiance, and it wouldn't be right to leave out the twin's Anger and Revenge. Yep! We were all there, waiting on God to give us a five-minute miracle. I had not yet learned the meaning of the word "process."

August 4, 2002

Dear Lord,

I give thanks in everything. After hearing the Word of God, I feel renewed in my spirit. Jesus, I love you through your Word. My passion is for your Word. Why? Because I learn about you and what you like and dislike. I am learning what moves you and how to get you to respond to me. I feel as if the Word is speaking directly to me, telling me to keep going and that I am on the right track. Jesus, there is something mysterious about you that makes me want to know more. I know you care about my character because you tell me not only what's wrong but also how to fix it. I can trust your Word. I know that you would not try to trick me. When it comes to people, I am a bad judge of character, but when it comes to you, I don't have to worry about being abandoned or about your being disloyal to me. You always have my best interest at heart. I've noticed that I talk to myself a lot. I have finally figured out why. I am answering the Holy Spirit after you have spoken to me.

Chapter Three

It had now been five months since my ex-husband had left. I thought that I was making progress. I had every tape I could find on marriage. I was also listening to the word of God on daily basis. I had shut out the rest of the world including my daughters and my extended family; I felt as if they didn't quite understand where I was spiritually as well as emotionally. The enemy loves to trick us into thinking we are the only ones who are living right for Christ and that no one before you or that will come after you will ever feel the pain you feel. In spite of the things that I wrote in my journal, I was still very sick. If you have ever given birth to a child maybe you can relate to what I am about to say. After you have come home from the hospital you don't mind being in the house for a while, but after a week or so, "cabin fever" sets in so you decide a trip to the grocery store is just the thing you need. After about the time it takes you to park the car and walk into the store, you realize you are not well. No one could have told you any different. It was something you had to learn on your own. Sometimes we can be that way spiritually. I am not trying to discount God's healing power in our lives, but he has so much more work he wants to do in our hearts, and that takes time. Are there any women out there like me that want a five-minute miracle? I was in such a hurry. After all, I was thirty-five years old, and "time was a wasting."

August 5, 2002

God told me if I were obedient to Him, I would get my husband back. It doesn't appear that my husband loves me anymore. He has told several of our friends he just wasn't happy with me. I am sure he misses his old friends and his extended family. He has it all, an apartment on the lake! What could be better than that? But God is in the "marriage-saving business."

Nothing could have prepared me for the events of the next two and one-half years of my life because I had a promise from God. On the other hand, did I? Regardless of whether I did or didn't, I was not going to let go! Prophetess eventually became weary of me. I guess she thought after months of ministry with me, the least I could do was get over this man. She began to tell me that "God had picked someone just for me." So now, I was faced with a whole new torment, my ex-husband or the mystery man God had waiting for me? **Hint: *"God is not the author of confusion."***

August 14, 2002

It seems the summer went by so quickly. Yet time seems to move so slowly, at least in my heart, when it comes to Shawn and me. No one knows better than I that it is a process and that we must endure. I pray to God that it does not take two years for Shawn and me to get remarried. My heart misses his hugs and his smile, and my bed misses his warmth. I think I would let him lie as close to me as he wanted to. Oh, how my heart aches for his warm hands and gentle touch....

I learned a lot last night about a man's self-esteem from the tapes on marriage. My dad had tried to tell me how to treat my husband, that I had to make him feel like a man, but I had been clueless to what he meant. I would get mad at him and say, "I do everything to please him! I don't know how much more of a man I can make him feel!" I was so sadly mistaken. I didn't realize that every negative word I said about the house and the yard, about his not being the best handyman, and about the kids and the coffee shop all wore away at his pride and manhood. Because he was ignoring me, I thought that he didn't care or that he was just being irresponsible. Well, he was responding, but not in my favor.

I feel as if I killed him, emotionally. I have cried so many tears for the hurts I caused him. I feel as though I have "trampled my family to death" with my silly goals. What good is it to have dreams if they will cost me my husband, my family, and God? A wife should be loyal to her family first. She is supposed to be the giver. She must find joy in serving her family's needs, or she could find herself without anyone to serve, as I found out this summer. The kids are with their dad, and I miss them very much.

O.K., the pity party is over! God, help me not to give place to the Devil. Only you deserve the glory for the things you have done. God, thanks for being my deliverer from depression, sorrow, and loneliness! God, I thank you that Shawn loves the girls.

Summer would soon be gone, and fall would be upon me. I was still full of hope that my ex-husband was on his way home to me. I continued to seek God everyday to the best of my knowledge. I pretended that I had joy and was a regular at the altar every Sunday. On Sundays, my time was divided between

Prophetess's church and my church in Indianapolis, IN. I felt as though I needed both. When I went to Prophetess's church, she would minister to others as well as me, one person at a time. That was fine with me. However, because my kids felt lost and very uncomfortable, I began to feel guilty. So I decided to alternate church visits from week to week.

Meanwhile, Prophetess became my best friend, and we spent time together every day. She would tutor my kids after school at her daycare at no charge as well as help me financially. In my eyes, she could do no wrong. My family members were not as fond as I was of her, but they knew I was on the verge of a nervous breakdown and she was the one who lived closest to me. Therefore, she became my family. Since my girls were with their dad almost every weekend, I had lots of free time on my hands.

To ward off my loneliness, I would spend the weekends with Prophetess and her husband. Since I had little money, I could no longer travel or shop, my two favorite pastimes. After a while, I started to become increasingly lonely, in spite of my friendship with Prophetess. She had her husband: I was sick of being the third wheel! So I began to petition God again about my marriage. I knew that October 6, which would have been our 10th anniversary, would soon be here, so I begged God to let that date be a turning point in our lives. I guess I was asking God to put us back together by that date.

August 19, 2002

I declare first things first – my total obedience to God and total healing from the past. Yokes have been broken and given to God. Hearts have been healed, and my marriage has been restored in Heaven as it is in earth. I command by the authority that is given by Jesus Christ, the Son of the living God, that Shawn will return home to me on October 6, 2002. He will be made whole. He will be set free to serve God with his whole heart. He will be able to love the girls and me with a godly wisdom. We will prosper in Christ and win souls to Christ as a family that has survived divorce.

I had become delusional in my Christian walk. All of my efforts were centered on getting my marriage back. I really thought I was doing the right thing – and I was – but for the wrong reason. There were so many things that I did not understand about God. I had been raised to pray and have faith that God would do what we asked Him to do. That may have been the case in the late seventies, but God was trying to bring me to a higher understanding of Him. He wanted me to really know Him. I had the "faith department" pretty much licked, but there was a big difference between having "faith in what God can do" and having "faith to trust that God knows what is best for me." The difference was a little word called "surrender."

Funny, I thought that I had surrendered. To what, I was not sure because my will had not yet aligned itself with God's will for my life. To break it down for you, "I was stuck on stupid!" I believe Prophetess knew that, but she had not planned on my staying there long. I began to frustrate her with my insistent assertions that Shawn was the man for me. Sometimes, it is really hard when one is trying to win another to Christ. Often, the lure used is the very thing that God has removed from that person's life. If someone is led to believe that God is going to do something He never said He would do, when God begins to reveal His perfect will for that person's life, it is hard for that person to make the transition from his or her own desires to God's plan for his or her life.

August 22, 2002

God, I know you are the God of second chances, and I love you for that. My circumstances have not changed one bit, but my life has been renewed, cleansed, and made whole. The hurt is very faint, if not gone. If I chose to pick up that pain, I'm sure that it can be arranged, but I choose to leave those things in the past and press toward the mark. What is the mark of God's high calling for my life? I pray for Shawn's healing and for his soul to be saved quickly. I feel as if my life is like a horse and buggy that are out of control and I am holding the reins. I want Shawn to hurry and catch up and take the reins. I don't know how much longer I can keep control. The house, the bills, the kids! With everything going on, I really don't have time to be lonely, or am I really lonely? Jesus has taken the loneliness away. "Thank you, Jesus, but I still want Shawn here with us. I want him to look at his family and smile and say without a doubt, "I love them."

We would say in return, "We love you, too."

I really don't think the sex thing has bothered me too much. God, did you temporarily relieve me of that burden? You said you would not put more on me than I can bear. I guess only God knows, but I want it back when "my baby" gets home.

August 23, 2003

Well, it's Friday, and God is worthy to be praised. Prophetess told me to take Shawn my bills that I couldn't pay. I did and he agreed to pay them. He was so sweet about it. He is keeping the girls this weekend. I find it strange that the very things that I always wanted to do with him; he is now doing with the girls, but "no negative vibes, Baby." I will get my chance soon. I thank God I had a little money left over this week. I kept going over my bills, and I kept coming up on the positive side. God, you are so good to me, even when I am restless and miss Shawn.

During this time in my life, I was still very confused. One minute, I was praising God for healing me and making me whole; the next, I was begging Shawn to hurry up and come home. By now, I am sure you are beginning to wonder what the deal is with this "prophetess woman." Only time will tell. **Note: "*Hindsight is always 20/20.*"** As the days dragged on, I became very self-critical. I thought Shawn was a saint and I should worship the ground he walked on. He became the thing I worshiped more than God himself. There was so much truth in the things that God was showing me about myself. I could not see that a good marriage required the efforts of both partners. I blamed myself for everything. I began to ask God specific questions.

August 25, 2003

Questions and requests:

1. How should I conduct myself in Shawn's presence?

2. How can I tell when a trial is coming close to an end?

3. Sometimes, I think I have been made whole, and then I think that I am not. How do I know the difference? Lord, please give me clarity.

I believe that God, in due time, will give me the answers to my questions through His Word. Lord, I just need more Word. The more Satan attacks me, the more broken I become before you. My trials fuel the fire, and that is what makes me pure.

At this time, God was really working behind the scenes in my life. I could not see it then, but God was giving me revelation through my writing in my journal. You see, sometimes God will send us an encouraging word, but we twist it to fit our own purposes for our lives. When we do this, God's purpose cannot be fulfilled in our lives because we have not surrendered to His perfect will for our lives. We can never emotionally blackmail God through His Word by saying, "God, you said "this" and "that." Chances are we have misinterpreted what He was really trying to tell us. I cannot speak for others, but through my journal, I know that is what was happening to me.

During those months of waiting, I was constantly in the Word of God. As I said, He had a purpose for everything that He was taking me through. I would listen to tapes on how to get close to God. I thought that listening to them would hurry the process along. I did not know how to rest in the process, but God showed me how, and I will tell you what God told me later on in this book. Meanwhile, God was laying foundations that He knew I would put in this book. These are the building blocks that will put others on the right path of recovery. Remember, the Devil wants us to think we will never recover, but God says if we are obedient to His Word and seek His face…not His hand, we will have a full recovery and a good life.

September16, 2002

Wow! It's the middle of September already! Where did this miserable year go? Who cares! I thank you, God, for church today. As usual, it was very inspiring …. I have been a little frustrated with Shawn. I don't want to become ungrateful for what God has done. Shawn always returns my calls when I call. I just wish he wasn't so cold to me. I believe he would do anything for us. God, I thank you for that, but at times I would trade a hundred dollars for a kind word or smile….

September 17, 2002

I talked to Prophetess today. She said that Oct. 6 was too soon. I agreed with her because I wouldn't want to marry his crabby old tail anyway! He was testing my waters to see if I was going to roast him. It really did test my faith because he was so mean to me. He made me want to fire him up just one good time. Yes, Lord, I can see why we are not ready to be together. My flesh needs to die! Die! Die!

On the lighter side of things, Lord, I thank you for spending the morning with me. I danced before the Lord. It was total freedom. Then I went into worship. Jesus, I love being with you. There is a song that says, "More than life to me." Then there is another song that says, "Your love is life to me." Yet still another song says, "Your love is better than life...."

There is something about Jesus or just being in His presence. It is where time stops and life begins. Jesus, I love your Word. It gives me joy! I was thinking about when God calls us forth in the battle for souls. I thought about Wonder Woman and the way that super heroes respond to their mission. First of all, Wonder Woman has to put on her gear. She has the helmet of salvation, which sort of looks like a crown or tiara. She has on her belt of truth. It is gold like her crown. Next, she has on her bracelets which are her shield of faith. You know how we women are: Everything has to be in pairs. And don't forget her red boots of peace. Though it is a little skimpy, she is wearing her breastplate of righteousness. She is missing one thing, her sword of the spirit, which is the Word of God. When she goes to get her assignment, the first thing she is told is what she needs to do. Next, she asks to see footage on the enemy. Then, she is asked if she is capable of completing the mission. She replies, "It's going to be difficult, but I believe I can do it. She never says it can't be done. "Through Christ, all things are possible."

I was enjoying my time with the Lord. He was preparing me for what was to come. This was a season of peace for me. I did not see the stormy seas ahead. All I could see was my future with Shawn and how sad I was without him. I once heard my pastor say, "The Lord never gives us back old things that He has taken away. He said in His word, "*Behold, all things become new.*" I was still holding onto Shawn because that was what I was supposed to do – have faith, right? Why is it so hard to see what God's will is for our lives? I suppose we want things to go our way and still be in God's will.

The reason why I am sharing this part of my journal is that I want others to understand that whenever God takes something away from them or whenever He allows a relationship to be severed, they should ask themselves why He would allow things to happen this way. They should also ask themselves, "Am I putting this person or relationship above God?"

I know when I first met Shawn, I had so much hurt and baggage from my late teens and early twenties that the first thing I needed was to heal from those past relationships, and the last thing I needed was yet another relationship. When I was growing up, I always had a boyfriend. I couldn't imagine not having someone in my life. I continued that pattern all throughout my adult life until God finally said, "You need to chill!"

Well, chilling wasn't working for me. I was lonely, and I was becoming impatient. What do you think the two main things that God wanted to work out in me were? If you said patience and perseverance, you were correct. I was willing to wait as long as I still had hope that God would put Shawn and me back together. I could not imagine God doing things any other way. I believe that when God starts working on the inside of us, He has to remove a lot of "junk" and old habits that have become second nature to us, whether it is living in sin or a simple thing like not being accountable to anyone but ourselves.

I had not noticed the subtle changes in my life over the years. My life had been so confined as a child. I had grown up in a two-parent Apostolic home. Don't get me wrong: I had wonderful parents, but when I became a teenager, everyone else was wrong but me. I remember thinking like most young people, "I can't wait to be grown so I can do what I want and I don't have to answer to anyone but myself." Well, I carried that mental attitude into my adult life, even though I knew the Bible said, "*You are not your own but are bought with a price.*" I honestly thought I could be saved and selectively serve God. "What do you mean by that?" you ask. Well, instead of asking God, "What is your will for my life?" I would do what I wanted to do, and when things in my life began to fall apart, I would ask God to fix it or to "bless my mess!" I lived my whole adult Christian life that way all the way up until I was 35 years old. So you see, all my thought patterns had to be reset by God. This can prove to be a very long and frustrating process.

This book is intended to be a catalyst to making your transition less frustrating than mine has been. The faster you learn to surrender to God, the faster healing will begin to manifest in your life.

September 18, 2002

Lord, I have been fighting a kind of sadness in my heart... I cried out this morning in prayer. God, it seemed different. I didn't feel full or satisfied with our time together. God, I have been spoiled by your presence. I can't go a day without attention from you. You have my full attention. I need your time, love, and attention. You complete me, Jesus. I am very lonely, and I depend on Prophetess to be there, but, Jesus, you are the only one I can call on and talk to 24 hours a day. I wish I didn't feel this way, and I don't... all the time. I feel as though there is a lot of pressure on me right now. God, please don't pull away or hold back. I need your strong presence. I saw Shawn today. I miss him so much. I miss the boy I met 10 years ago. I also miss the man I married. The last nine years seem like a blur. Dad said that if we get remarried again, he would pay for our wedding. I don't think he believes that we are getting back together. Neither does anyone else. Everyone is like "Okey Dokey!" all except Prophetess and Ashley (my youngest daughter). I imagine I sound really foolish....

September 19, 2002

God, you said, "In everything give thanks." So, Lord, I thank you for everything that you have done in Shawn's life and mine. I repent if I have in anyway shown you doubt or ungratefulness for the things you have done for me. I am sorry. As a mother, I know it hurts when you do the best you can for your children and they are ungrateful. I am sure the grief you feel is the same or, perhaps, a million times worse when all of your children are whining and complaining about what we don't have, instead of giving thanks for what we do have. You are off the hook, Jesus! I love writing love letters to you. You are the love of my life. You are so wonderful. I thank you for your presence today. Feelings change from day to day, but your touch is what I crave and long for. I love to just lie before you and cry as I listen to the words of each song. I cannot always express how I feel, but the Spirit makes intercession.

Today, I didn't know what to pray for, but I must have been praying for someone.... If only I could just grasp the idea that this is your way of dealing with my spirit man, when I am having feelings of loneliness and doubt…! God is trying to let me know that all of this drama is leading up to something much greater than my momentary sadness and brokenness.

God, the pages in this tablet are coming to an end. I thank you for my journey and for giving me positive people, prayer warriors, and women of peace. God, you are incredible! I look around and see that you have put me in a garden that I can eat from. There are so many wonderful fruits.

Fall would soon be here. There is something about going into a new season that gives us a renewed since of hope. We often relate a new season of the year with God's bringing us into a new season of our life. However, this is not always the case. The reality of this idea totally depends on whether God feels we are ready to step into that new season that He has prepared for us. I remember feeling as though I was ready for change. I was so sick of just waiting on God to change my circumstances. I would stress myself out in prayer, trying to find out from God, "What is it that you want from me? Haven't I suffered enough?" I could not understand why God had to be so difficult. Why couldn't He just fix my circumstances and let me live my life? I told God, "I have learned my lesson, so please give me back my life." I was 35 years old; yet, sometimes, I felt like a newborn in Christ. I had to start all over again, and I hated that idea.

Does this have a ring of familiarity? How many times have you been in an unhealthy, ungodly relationship and knew that it needed to end? Did you find yourself making excuses about why you should stay in the relationship? The number one reason I had usually heard from my friends and family was, "I don't want to start over."

There is this great fear of the unknown, and rightfully so! Personally, I would always imagine my future worst than my past had been. This undesirable, imaginary situation would help me to relieve myself of the guilt that I felt when God was trying to call me out of "my mess." I always thought my relationship with God was like SAFE AUTO INSURANCE: I just wanted "minimum coverage" because full coverage would cost me too much. God was just too demanding of me. He wanted things from me that I just was not ready to give up just yet. I had my own idea of how things should be. I would pray, and He would answer "yes" or "no" because that is what I thought, I was supposed to do. This starting over thing was just way too much. It was why I had to keep repeating the same process over and over. Come to think of it, wasn't that the same as starting over?

September 20, 2002

Praise be to God, another week has gone by quickly! I thank God for His miracles this week. I cannot help but to think of Shawn. He is always in my thoughts. I believe he still loves me. Before, there was such coldness in his heart, but now it seems the ice is melting off his heart. I wish I had a blow dryer – I would help him out! I guess I will have to learn to go on until that day comes. It seems different when I write. I don't seem to have all the drama that I had in the past. This has been a peaceful time for me. Father, I thank you for a season of peace. Well, it is time to pray about my weight. In the name of Jesus, I curse the demons of oppression that come against my body, the hunger demons, and the laziness demons. I command you to go, in Jesus' name. I will lose weight, be active, and keep my house clean.

There were parts of my journals that I felt were non-essential. While I was proofreading them, I came across the entry that you have just read. I felt you needed some comic relief, so I included it. The sad part about it is I think I was serious about casting out those hunger and lazy demons!

Chapter Four

September 24, 2002

Well, I just came back inside from seeing Shawn. The Lord is so faithful towards me with His kindness. I will never understand God's acts of kindness. When the pressure is on, God always gives me a taste of His glory and of what is to come. He meets me at the point of my needs. I really don't know what happened. I didn't mean to complain to Shawn, but it seemed to end up that way. I do have faith, and I have used it. I guess I wanted some encouragement from Shawn. God, I know you understand.

I will wait on the Lord and be of good courage. Jesus, I love you! I have a lot of growing up to do, Jesus. Thank you for putting up with me and for being able to see the beginning from the end. I don't know what kind of ministry you have in store for me. Because from where I stand, I cannot imagine my life being any different. By faith, I will not carry this hurt and baggage any further. I am a new creature in Christ, and by faith, I will make intelligent choices and will not always struggle from week to week.

I was very much still struggling in my Christian walk, and I was hurting so badly. All I had was the Word on which I had grown up, and it was limited to the familiar scriptures that I had heard over the years of being at my home church New Bethel

Tabernacle. Nevertheless, I fought with all that was in me to stay encouraged and to use what I knew. God loved me enough to let me struggle, and through my struggles, I would one day become strong.

September 30, 2002

Well, it's Sunday night, and this week has gone by very quickly. This past weekend was the NBT Women's Retreat. Prophetess went with me. I was looking forward to going. I asked God to allow Prophetess to minister, and she did. The first night she danced to "Alabaster Box." I was sure she was going to give that box to Sister Jones. When she got close to the end of the song, everyone was crying, including me. I was so proud of her. But when she brought the box to me, I could have cried, and I did! I don't think that she knew what that did for me. She has loved me like no other friend, unconditionally, with her whole heart. She made me feel so special. I am so honored to be her friend. However, just when things were looking up, the Old Serpent, the Devil, showed up, trying to undo all that God had done that night. Prophetess held her ground and her peace. I didn't, but no matter what I said, she didn't let it get to her. I am in awe of her and the gifts God has given her. People always crack under pressure and their true nature shows. She had true character! I am working on that as I write. I always thought that it could not be done, but she is a true witness that it can be done. To God be the glory for the things He has done! We stayed up all night, still having fun, talking about nothing and everything just like sisters.

September 31, 2002

Shawn brought the girls home. Earlier that week, he had helped me with the van. He actually looked me up and down. Before, I could not even get him to look me in the eyes much less anywhere else. Today, when I talked to him, he seemed so different...so much nicer. Thank you, Jesus, for answering my request. I can hear you say, "Consider it done!" And I do....

    P.S.: *I can't wait for my wedding ....*

As I read my journal, my heart saddened at the state of mind I was in. There were times when I considered leaving out the really stupid things that I wrote like "my wedding." It was painful to revisit that time in my life. However, it was necessary that I do so in order that others might be able to relate to how I was feeling and thinking. I pray that when you begin to help others in your own ministry and walk with Christ, you will have compassion on them, and remember where God has brought you from.

When I first started my recovery process, my thoughts were so black and white. All I had to rely on was my past. I could not foresee the awesome future that God had in store for me. That was why I chose to look back instead of forward. When I did decide to look forward, I saw only *my* own plans, not God's. I did not know what God's plans were, and that was scary to me. Therefore, I made up my own. It made me feel as if I were in control.

October 1, 2002

Can you believe it is October already? Sunday would have been 10 years for Shawn and me. I must face it with joy and believe that it will get better. I thought that Shawn and I would have been further along. I guess in some ways we are, and I thank God it's not as bad as it used to be. I needed money, so I called Shawn and asked him for one hundred dollars, and then I considered it done. He acted a little hesitant, so I told him, "That's O.K.," and with that, he changed his mind. I thank God for using him as a provider. It feels strange, yet I know God is running things. I love it when God doesn't make sense. That means He is up to something. Even so, I hate asking Shawn for money. I feel as though it makes him hate me all the more – "The begging ex-wife!" Nevertheless, God is using an awkward situation to build character in me, to cause Shawn to love through giving, and to increase my faith.

October2, 2002

October? Where did the time go? Wherever it went, thank God it went! I have become restless in my soul, and I think I am ready to fight. I hate to say this, but I'm getting a little bored. I think God tends to bore us to death when our flesh must die and His will must begin. Let's use, for an example, a solider in the army who has already been through basic training. He is on his first mission, and the sergeant tells him to lie low for a while. At first, he feels relief. But after a while, he grows tired of staying in the same place, and he begins to itch for battle because he wants the battle to be over so he can move on to the next assignment. Well, that is how I am starting to feel. I feel like I have been in the trenches too long.

I listened very carefully to the prophetic CD that Prophetess had made me...over and over again. I began to notice small things that Prophetess was saying to be true, for example, the crying of tears. I have cried so hard these past few days. I cannot explain why. I didn't feel sad. The enemy had tried to tell me it was due to my anniversary coming up on Sunday, but I didn't accept that because it wasn't sorrow I felt. It was love for Jesus and the longing to touch His feet. I just long more and more to be in His presence. It's never enough. I cannot explain it. I hunger for Him. That is why I wept. It was as if I expected to actually touch Jesus' feet. How strange.... I guess my time with God is starting to change. It feels more like worship instead of asking God for things. He has already made me promises. Lord knows, rushing Him does not work. I can feel myself changing; the fear is going away. For God I live, and for God I die! What else is there?

I like this entry because I knew that God was drawing me nearer to Him. I was so sick in my heart. I don't think I was any different from any other person going through a divorce because such a person understands the great pain that is felt and carried. However when I am in God's presence, there is no pain. It ceases to exist. It is just Jesus and me. I felt as though it was the only time when my heart did not ache for Shawn. Therefore, I stayed there as long as I could. God's presence was where healing began to take place in my heart. When I did leave His presence, my faith was renewed.

God's presence reminds me of manna in the Old Testament: We cannot keep it until the next day. We have to go into His presence everyday to get a fresh dose of His healing power. Unfortunately, we choose to take God like two aspirins whenever we feel pain, then, put Him back in our purse, and carry Him around until we get another headache. God was trying to show me a different way of dealing with my pain. I believe that was why my faith sometimes wavered back and forth so much.

In the past, I would just pray and throw a holy temper tantrum when I wanted something. That was what I was used to doing. Sometimes it worked, but it was not helping me to grow up and to learn that not everything was about me. Even though I had been raised in church my whole life, the way that God was now dealing with me was all new to me.... I was still a big, over-grown baby! **"Hind sight is 20/20."** It is easier to look back at someone else's mistakes and relate than it is making one's own mistakes, and it is a lot less painful. This is why I am sharing mine with you, no matter how embarrassing the situation is.

As I reviewed my journal, I realized that I had written many things that had not always made sense. I was blind to God's purpose for my life. I believed that God's healing me was a one-time deal and that there was something wrong with my spiritual life on those days when I did not feel well. That was what I had been taught all my life. That was why it was so important for me to keep these Journals. They allowed me to keep track of my good days and helped me to understand that my bad days were only temporary. Therefore so are yours!

I will probably repeat some things in this book, for example, the fact that God was using my journal as a spiritual tool by which to measure my growth. One day, I felt as if I could take on the world, whereas the next day, I wondered how I was going to climb out of bed. I began to see a pattern in my writings. I also began to notice the dates and times of each month when I would experience the highs and lows: There were times when I felt sad and unable to bare another disappointment. I later learned that some of those low moments were due to my hormones, but I still like to give God all the glory for bringing me through.

We females like to refer to that time of the month as PMS. It causes things such as rejection, bills, and hardheaded children to appear more life threatening than they really are. If you are a male, I'm not sure what to tell you, but I promise to be nice. So as you read the journal sections of this book, take note of the dates: I tend to go off the deep end around the same time of every month. I guess I said all that to say this: Not everything is the Devil. Sometimes it is just us.

October 4, 2002

Two days before my dreaded 10-year anniversary! I have tried not to cry, and, so far, I have been O.K. Shawn seems to be agitated. I'm not sure why? I just tell myself, "It's test time again." If I can love him when he's acting evil, it won't be hard to love him when he's nice. I'm not quite sure about the time, but I feel like God is saying it's going to be a year from the day Shawn left. Now if He had said that when Shawn first left, I would have died!

Wow, it is so funny how we know God better than He knows himself! I spent way too much time trying to predict what He was going to do. I believe a lot of this came from the time I spent with Prophetess. I hung onto her every word. In fact, I became a prophetic junkie. It was easier to try to figure out what God was going to do than to walk by faith. That was funny! I thought I had the faith department licked. Oh, yes, this was blind faith, so, of course, this was different! I could not pray my way out of this trial.

I was locked down. There was no way out this time. I felt since God was making me go this way, I deserved an explanation to what was going on with my life. So when He didn't give me an answer, I would worry Prophetess to death, and bombard her with questions. She didn't have the heart to tell me the truth, because she was hoping that I would change my mind about Shawn and move on with my life. That is the bad thing about baiting someone with something God is trying to remove from his or her life. There's no growth, and that person begins to sound like a broken record. Shamefully, I admit that, based on the level

29

of faith people did or did not have, I myself have told them what they wanted to hear…as if God had said it. Instead, they needed to be reminded that God was in control, even if it seemed as if they were falling apart. **Hint: It is O.K. to say, "I don't know. You will have to just trust God."**

October 5, 2002

Well, it's Friday night. I am here by the grace of God. I have one more thing to add to my grateful list. Instead of sorting parts, my boss let me run my job. Yeah! I had an encounter on the internet earlier. It wasn't about the person I had met. It was about the person I've become. As I was talking to this person, I didn't feel the need to impress him, only the need to be holy, not to make him feel bad, just to let him know that I stood for Jesus. The conversation began to stray, but I brought it back to focus. I was trying to get off the computer so I could go to work. He asked me to stay on line, but I had to go. It felt good to walk away and not feel so needy and desperate.

To tell the truth about how I feel, I have locked myself up and shut people out for so long. I pray that I will become more social. It's hard to be social when God is all you want. Good Lord! I've become Sister Super-Christian! Ha! Ha! Lord, I need to do better! Sometimes, I just don't know what to do with myself. I talked to Dad today. He seemed very interested in what Prophetess had to say. He said he would cancel his trip. Wow! God you are awesome!

It has been seven months since Shawn left. I must evaluate my relationship with him. Why does he seem so distant at times and so nice at others? Am I the one who is dealing with rejection issues? Lord, please help me to understand when I am the one or when I'm just reading him wrong. For example, when he calls me, he says, "Hey!" But when I call him, he says, "Yeah!" as though he can't say, "Hi" or

"Hello." It makes me feel as if he doesn't even want to be friends or anything with me. I will try not to take it personally. He may think he doesn't love me, but he will...I think the real reason why I haven't moved on is that I'm afraid of messing up God's promises for my life or afraid I'll step into disobedience. It is really hard to explain to people about my situation with Shawn when I don't always understand it myself. I find myself sounding like an idiot talking about him. I really don't want to sound too negative or too happy either, so I shy away from people. Lord, prepare me for what lies ahead, shield and protect me, please, in Jesus' name I pray. Amen.

O.K., I have been thinking, "Why do I feel so miserable?" I love God with my whole heart. I spend time with Him everyday. I live according to His ways. I believe it is because I do not fit in anywhere. I don't feel single, but I'm not married. I'm not supposed to love my husband anymore, but I do. We are supposed to be friends, but we're not. This is a difficult time in my life. I'm very lonely, and I don't want to be needy toward the people I love. It makes my heart ache to be around people who are married; it seems to remind me of how incomplete I feel. I can't flirt with or dream of anyone else because I'm promised to a person that doesn't even know he is supposed to love me. Where do I fit in?

All right, I know I have some explaining to do. I know it is hard to follow my journal completely because it seems to jump from one subject to another at times. That is because it is a journal! And...I was half crazy...out of my mind! I want to explain about my promise.

During my counseling sessions, I was going back and forth. I could not decide whether to move on or to wait for Shawn. My thoughts were black and white. I also believed that waiting for him gave me a sense of hope. It was a lot more scary facing the world without a false security, so I clung to the hope I had, no matter whether it made sense or not. I felt that the hope I had helped me to bear the pain of my loss. It was all I could do to function.

However, my false foundation was cracking. I could not accept the idea of being alone. It was too painful. My abandonment issues had not been dealt with yet, so it was Shawn or the unknown. You bet you, I chose to hold onto what was familiar to me. I was so frustrated with my choice, but I felt this was the only one I had.

Wait a minute! Didn't the word **choice** involve more than one direction? Didn't having choices mean we were able to move forwards as well as backwards? Then why do we choose to go backwards? If we were not moving forward, we were not making progress. That was why I felt so miserable, in spite of all my praying and lying before the Lord. I was like a CD that skipped in one place because it was damaged in that one particular place. It sounded O.K. until it got to that one area; then it just got stuck and repeated the same thing over and over. How annoying! As for my promise, the only promise God had made to me was the only one I needed, "***Plans to prosper you and to give you an expected end.***" Why was it so hard to believe? Maybe it was due to being lied to in the past by the ones who claimed to love me the most. What I needed to realize is that God could not lie, and that he truly loved me the most.

Cont… This is why I stay home and keep to myself. I am too holy for some, and others seem to know what I am going though, even though they have never been divorced. Prophetess is the only one who seems to understand me or even cares about what I have to say. God, I need help. I'm not sure where my focus belongs. I listen to CD's and watch TBN to death. I'm not discouraged. I just feel misplaced. My kids know I'm not happy. I think I make them sad. I don't want to keep them from their friends, but I also don't want them hanging around the wrong crowd. Lord, I need answers so I can function and not be living in vain. Help me to prepare for what it is you have for me. I feel like I'm lost. I have come so far, and now I have hit a plateau. Please jumps-start my life. Because I'm not allowed to know a time frame. I feel as if I'm swinging in the wind. I'm not even sure of what to say to Shawn besides "Hi, I need some money, Honey." I'm even sick of hearing my own voice. Jesus, I love you so much, but the silence hurts so much. When are things going to change? I hope I don't sound ungrateful because I'm not. Shawn has done superficial things. Thank you, Lord, but I need more before I drive my kids and Prophetess crazy from loneliness. What am I not grasping?

It's so funny when you are not familiar with the road you're traveling; the journey can seem so long and scary. It is the fear of being lost, or it could be the fear that you are going in the wrong direction. It has actually been seven years since I wrote this entry. So much has happened in those seven years. I will get to that part later on in this book, but I will tell you this: God planned every one of those seven years out. He made room for my failures because He knew in advance that I would fail. Remember Jeremiah 29: 11-13, **"For I know the plans that I have for you, declares the Lord. They are plans for peace and not disaster plans to give you a future, filled with hope and an expected end."** (NKJV)

Now, if God knew me before He formed me in my mother's womb, (Jeremiah 1:5 KJV) then He certainly had to know that I would lose both my husband and business and that I would be this deranged woman who thought every time the wind blew, it was a sign from God. He had to have known that I would feel lost and scared along the way as well as uncertain of my future. But how could it be that He would allow me to make so many mistakes and assumptions about Him or what He was going to do? I was making a complete idiot of myself. Why hadn't He stopped me?

Think about it, if God stopped every dumb thing a Christian did along his journey, there would be no testimonies. There would be no road map for others to follow, and there would be no laughter because, let's face it, I was hilarious! Not everyone is willing to admit his or her failures or that he or she missed God twenty miles back, but we all do, including King David, Moses, and Paul. That is why the Bible is so fabulous! It is our road map to life. It is our compass in the desert. After a while, everything begins to look the same – Sand is sand! – but the Bible is the compass, and the Word of God points us in the right direction in which to walk. Sometimes, it feels as if we haven't made much progress because in the desert, all sand looks the same, no matter how far we have walked in it. That is why it is necessary that we continue to seek the Word of God. Faith steps in through the Word of God. Whether we receive a word from reading our Bible or whether we receive a direct word from our pastor, I know God will send the Word to us.

October 6, 2002 (am)

Happy 10-year Anniversary! I could look at this as a great tragedy, but I choose to give my God all the glory and the praise. "In everything give thanks." The Word of God was so good today. I struggled this morning with whether to go to Indy or to stay home. I am so glad I went; God always knows what we need. This has been the most difficult time of my life, but God is teaching me things. I laugh at myself, at just how sensitive I am to the simple things, for example, when Shawn answers the phone "Yeah" instead of "Hello."

Last night, I watched a movie that had a lot of phone scenes. In these phone scenes, the person answered the phone "Yeah" at least 10 times. I just laughed. I guess I have been sensitive about Shawn's highs and lows. I guess the reason is I have only a few people in my life by which I can measure myself, Prophetess and the girls. I don't always seem to be the best judge of character, but I will be...by faith. I look at Prophetess. She is always smiling, and she is never in a bad mood, or at least she doesn't show it. I guess I expect everyone to behave like her, wrong! She had to set me straight on that.

Why is it so hard for me to see it? God, please open my eyes to see the difference between good and evil in a person? I guess I'm supposed to treat everyone good anyway. even, if I don't want a relationship with that person, but when my heart is sensitive because it already hurts, the least bit of pressure and ouch! I guess what I will accomplish through God, and the Holy Spirit is not to react to negative vibes, and to tune my heart to the Holy Spirit so that I can judge correctly on how to respond as a blood-brought saint. My opposition is my opportunity. I must grasp that in my spirit, and no matter how I feel, I must treat people in a Godly manner. Thank you, God, for growth.

There is a scripture that says, *"Out of the abundance of the heart the mouth speaks."* (Luke 6:5) I love this scripture because even though I was in a lot of pain, my heart was in the right place. I tried so hard to encourage myself by speaking to my situation. I didn't always make sense to everyone, but I made sense to God. He knew I was giving it my all. After all, I was a baby saint; this was my first trip around the mountain.

When my ex-husband Shawn would answer the phone, "Yeah," it would offend me because he was so cold towards me. When we were married, he never answered the phone that way. When one goes through a divorce, everything becomes a personal attack because nerves are raw. However, because the preacher tells us to rejoice in trials and tribulations, we feel as though our faith isn't strong enough or that there is something wrong with us because we're sad and depressed. Being sad and depressed is part of the process of healing, but wearing our problems on our head like a hat is not. Sadness is a feeling, not a lifestyle. Feelings come and go: Some days there is joy, and some days we just feel sad. Being sad does not mean we lack the faith to get better. The pain draws us closer to God because He is the only one that can subdue the pain. People become foreign to us when we are in great pain, and we become distant to them, too. Jesus is the only one that can truly relate to us when we are at that breaking point; it seems as if He allows us to go there. I have called friends and talked to them until I managed to make them as miserable as I was. I would go to bed crying and thinking, "God, if you don't help me, I am going to have a nervous breakdown." Then, I would wake up the next day, God would put His Word in my pathway by T.V. or radio, and it would be just what I needed from the Lord. Then, I would feel ashamed that I even complained to that person over the phone.

Because God allows us to suffer and go through the misunderstanding of life's problems, sometimes it does not seem possible that He hears our deepest concerns. We need to remember that there is no other way we will grow except through the growing pains. It is normal to think that we will always be miserable while we are sad, but Christ lets us know that this is only temporary, and "This, too, shall pass!" I was so down on myself. I was always afraid that I wasn't doing something right, and that is why God wasn't moving fast enough. However, I have learned that the slower God walks us through our trials, the more we become aware of ourselves and in relation to what God truly is to us. But wait! I have so much to share with you, but I don't want to get too far ahead of my journal.

October 7, 2002

Thank you, God! I survived! I didn't die on my anniversary. I thank you, God, for a good night and a wonderful day. I woke up at 3:45 this afternoon (I work midnights) and had just enough time to make it up to the school to help the girls with their lockers. Loren told me that she loved me so much. I said to her, "What's up?" She answered, "Nothing. I just love you so much."

No one except God will ever know how much that healed my heart and touched my soul. I thank you, God, for a child's love. I think this is the first time I have ever experienced it to the fullest, to where it was not being given, but received. God, you never cease to amaze me. You challenge me to grow.

I had so much going on in my life, yet it seemed like so little, or maybe it just seemed like time had simply stood still for a while. There is a two-and-one-half year gap before the next journal entries. It isn't that I didn't write during those two years because I distinctly remember writing during that time. I would pick a specific color for each journal according to my mood or season in my life. The first journal was yellow because I had a lot of fear when Shawn left. When that journal was filled up, I moved on to red because that was when I discovered that the blood of Jesus covered me. Unfortunately, the one journal I lost was black. When I picked black, I had no idea what I was about to walk into. I don't know if it was God's purpose for me to not include it in the book, but I believe *"all things work together for the good for those who are called according to His purpose."* (Romans 8:28)

PART TWO: "RITA"

Chapter Five

Although the names of my neighbors have been changed to protect their identity, the accounts I am about to tell you are all true. Although the stories are non-fiction, there were times when I felt like I was playing the leading role in my own Lifetime movie.

In 2000, two years prior to my divorce, I lived in an interesting neighborhood. Next door to me, lived some fascinating neighbors, a husband and his wife and two children. He was what one would consider a perfectionist. He kept his lawn immaculate, and he went so far as to put tacks on his front lawn to discourage kids from riding their bikes – accidentally, of course – through his lawn. At one time, he had used a pellet gun to shoot out the window of a person's car after the person continually parked his car in front of my neighbor's house. However, he was nice enough to tell the person, "Hey, your window is busted out!"

The neighbors across the street were an unmarried couple. The woman was addicted to drugs, and her boyfriend was addicted to alcohol. They were a recipe for trouble. Our peaceful little street was now one that was frequently filled with the sound of sirens and flashing red and blue lights. I had never before lived in a red light district until now. The man would beat the woman up, she would call the police, and they would take him to jail. Two weeks later, he would be out, she would take him back, and then the cycle would start all over again. After a while, this situation became the norm on our block.

One day, my daughter Ashley and I were almost ready to go to the store when I heard gun shots ring out. Hearing the sound of gunshots was foreign to me because I had never heard live gun shots before this incident. Paralyzed momentarily, I felt death in the air. When I finally gathered enough courage to look out the window, I saw nothing.

Fifteen minutes later, I heard the familiar sound of sirens. Again, I looked out my window, only to see my next-door neighbor being ushered into a police car. I thought to myself, "What has Bill done now?"

I told Ashley, "Get your coat on. We need to go pick up Loren from school."

We walked out our front door only to find a body in our front yard. I screamed, "Is he dead?" A few minutes later, the lifeless body was being put into a body bag. My front yard was taped off as a crime scene that day. This incident was, I believe, the closest I had ever come to death, someone being gunned down on my front lawn.

Later on, we would find out that Bill, my next-door neighbor, had murdered his wife's brother John. I learned that John, who had previously been released from the Michigan City prison, had been temporarily staying with his brother- in- law Bill, and his wife Lisa when the shooting occurred.

Two years later, I had no idea that I would be divorced and still living on this same street alone! One morning, I was driving home from work (remember, I worked midnights), and I saw someone who I thought was John sitting in Lisa's garage: The garage door was open. However, how could that be when John was dead! My heart was gripped with fear as I slowed my car and pulled into my driveway. Too afraid to utter a word, I hurried out of my car and into my house.

Later on that day, I asked my daughter, "Who is that over at Bill and Lisa's house?" She told me Lisa had another brother who had come to live with her to help her because Bill was now in jail and she was not mentally well.

Soon after what would have been our 10th anniversary, I began to lose hope that Shawn and I would ever be reunited. Though I continued to pray for our reunion, I was also vacillating between this reunion and the idea that God had this "Promised Man" in store for me. Meeting this man was now becoming more of a priority than praying for Shawn to come home. Unless I was in God's presence – "laid out" on the floor, crying, I felt torn, and I hurt all the time. To put it bluntly, I became very well acquainted with the carpet in my home.

The leaves had all fallen from the trees; winter was setting in, with its cold bitter winds. The girls and I spent Christmas with my mother and step-dad. (I only refer to him as my step-dad because my parents are divorced. He is the most wonderful, caring dad any child could ever be blessed to have.) This was my first Christmas without Shawn. In spite of his absence, the girls enjoyed their Christmas. They were given extra that year because my wonderful family decided to spoil them. I didn't mind; they deserved it.

It did not snow until after Christmas day, but it must have snowed all though the night because the next morning I was awakened to the sound of a snow blower. As I looked out my window, I saw Lisa's mysterious brother clearing my driveway. He never said a word, just cleared it, and went back next door. I was not dressed, so I did not open the door. I thought to myself, "That was very nice thing for him to do, especially after I had purposely avoided speaking to him for the last two months."

I did not know him, and, to tell the truth, he seemed a little bit strange to me. In spite of my reservations about this man, I decided to make a cookie tray for Lisa and her family to say thank you for clearing my driveway. I was sure that it had to have been extra hard on their family with Lisa's loss of both her brother and her husband…all in one day! Our kids, who were also schoolmates, played together everyday, so I actually saw no harm in giving them a plate of cookies; after all, that is what neighbors are for.

I sent the girls over with the cookies, and Lisa and her family enjoyed them. The next day, there was a knock on my front door. I looked through the peephole to see who it was. It was the mysterious man from next door! I felt very nervous, but I decided to open the door anyway. He introduced himself and said he was bringing back my plate.

I thanked him, but he just stood there. I asked him if he was the one who had cleared my driveway, and he replied, "Yes."

Again, I thanked him and told him, "Come in. It's cold outside." He did. He told me his name and said that he was a handy man, that he knew a lot about houses and construction, and if I ever needed anything fixed, just let him know. Then he left.

During this time, I was still going to church at both places, Prophetess's church on Grissom AFB and Overcoming Church in Indianapolis, IN. On this particular Sunday, I had decided to stay in Peru and go to Prophetess's church, and guess who showed up there, too. Yes, my neighbor from next door. I will simply call him Derrick. I was taken aback by his presence, but he did not seem surprised at all seeing me there.

Prophetess's services, I believe I mentioned earlier, were geared toward a smaller crowd. She normally praise danced, preached, and then prayed for everyone personally as well as ministered to whomever she felt needed it. Well, I suppose this was Derrick's Sunday. During the service, he seemed to be touched by the Word of God. He began to break down and cry. Derrick appeared as though he had lived a rough life. It showed in his face. Sin will always make you look older than you truly are.

For some reason, his tears really got to me, mainly – I believe – because I considered him to be a very intense man, the kind of man to whom I was attracted to along with all the drama that came with the intensity. This type of man always needed fixing, or he just needed someone to believe in him. The problem was who was going to fix her when she was broken because of him. (That is just something to think about.)

The following week, Derrick received Jesus Christ into his heart and gave his life to Christ. Week after week, Derrick would find some excuse to come by my house, whether it was to say hello or to borrow something. Regardless of the reason, he was there.

Our friendship grew quickly and began to blossom into what I thought was love. Right in the middle of it all, there was Prophetess, watching and observing but not interfering. I thought this unusual because she always had something to say about everything I did. Derrick was a model boyfriend at first; he had issues, but managed to convince me that they were not his fault. In spite of all that I knew about his past, I wasn't deterred from going out with him. I was sure that God would wipe the slate from his past clean, and he would magically become a new creature in Christ. I really believed in my heart that he was "my promise" from God.

Three months into our relationship, things seemed to be going great. I did not allow Derrick too much intimacy. We kept our dates in public places and tried to limit our physical touch for obvious reasons. In spite of all the precautions, it was still very difficult because he lived next door to me. I had been a married woman for almost ten years and was used to a physical relationship. That is the hard part about being divorced. However, when a person is living for Christ, he is not his own, and God holds him to a higher measure of accountability.

The longer we dated, the harder it became to keep our flesh under control. I say we because even if "he" was the aggressor, it takes two to tangle. The problem with dating is that a lot of time we can be unequally yoked with a man or a woman, from the beginning. It seemed as though I spent most of my time quoting scriptures to a person that did not know God, much less cared about what the Bible had to say about premarital sex. Yet, I thought he was saved. Now I am not one to judge another's salvation, but if an apple tree is growing lemons, it is probably a lemon tree, no matter how much it tells you it loves you, and that it is an apple tree. For some odd reason, however, I still believed he was an apple tree that just needed help to stop growing those darn lemons!

I remember having such lovely conversations with him. He would tell me about his family and the hardships of his childhood. We also talked about his ex-wife and why they were no longer married. It was all her fault according to him, and being a "good woman," I believed him. After all, he just needed someone that could love him the right way, even though he was somewhat mean. His temperament was just a product of his bad childhood and the way his ex- wife had treated him. Now that he had been saved for two whole months, God was supposed to wipe away all the damage from his past just like that. I guess it was his turn for a five-minute miracle.

Well, back in the day, that was what I was taught, and that was all I knew. When a person got saved, he was instantaneously changed. Today, we learn that there was a lot of "faking it" back then. Being saved is God's process of saving one from whatever sin he or she has been committing. It takes time, sometimes years, to learn how to be completely obedient to God. I know it was true for me. That is why it was foolish of me to think it was O.K. to be spiritually unequally yoked with this man.

Derrick had so many unresolved issues such as anger, hurt, and rage. Whether he was saved or not was not the issue. The real issue was that we were not in the same place on our salvation walk, and, to tell you the truth, I was still just as damaged as he was, only in a different way. Unfortunately, I did not think I needed anymore help. Besides, I was trying to help Derrick, and I was still oblivious to the fact that healing takes time. I just wanted to help Derrick so he could fix my pain of not being married. My source had transferred from Jesus to this man I hardly knew.

The reason I share this experience in detail with you is that I know there are so many young women and men who will think that they have found their soul mate. No matter how bad things actually get, they will make the mistake of not walking away from dysfunctional relationships for various reasons such as, "He needs me," or "If I leave him, he won't have anybody to love him," or "I can help strengthen his walk with Christ. I am strong enough for the both of us." Wrong! He will have Jesus to love him, and Jesus alone is sufficient. The fact that someone would even make these statements demonstrates a lack of spiritual maturity. Mature Christians know the Word of God tells us, "*Be not unequally yoked with unbelievers.*" (II Corinthians 6:14)

The pressure of Derrick's wanting to sleep with me was more than I could bear, so after my many attempts to correct his behavior, I broke up with him. At first, he was very angry with me, but I suppose that because I ignored his tantrums, he finally decided to try a different approach: He became a very well behaved gentleman. I began to miss him, so I gave in and decided he deserved another chance. Well, it wasn't too long after that, that he asked me to marry him. I thought, "Yes, this is my promise from God!" Prophetess knew about my relationship with Derrick because she was his pastor at the church he and I attended. Of course, I told her everything, anyway.

When she asked me, "Are you sure this is who you want to marry?" I would have a dumb look on my face, as if I knew better, but didn't care. I wanted her to slap me and tell me, "Are you crazy, girl? Can't you see this man is crazy?" But she didn't.

I would go to her and complain about Derrick constantly, but she never outright said to me, "Leave him alone." She would just ask, "Are you sure you want to marry this man?"

I took her reactions as a green light to go, without looking both ways before I crossed that intersection. I suppose I was attracted to the idea of being married more than I was mindful of the consequences of being married to the wrong man. I honestly thought that God would fix Derrick. My faith was distorted by my desire to be with this man, no matter what anyone told me. I had a hard heart, even though I was saved. I know that sounds unbiblical as well as crazy, but that is the only way to describe how I felt. I loved God, but I wanted what I wanted, and I twisted the Gospel to fit into my plans. God did try to warn me, but I thought everyone was wrong and I was right, and this was what God wanted me to do, even if it didn't look like or sound like God.

The night before we got married, Derrick and I got into to a huge fight because he wanted to have sex. He said, "What does it matter if we are getting married tomorrow?" At that point, I was ready to end our relationship – and I should have – but I felt so ashamed that I had fought with my Dad and my brother about Derrick that my pride kept me from doing what I knew was right.

Before I continue with my story about Derrick, I want to encourage you to not be afraid to tell a friend if you feel he or she is headed towards a train wreck, especially if you are in a place of mentorship or leadership. Sometimes, that person needs to hear a confirmation of what God has already spoken to his or her spirit, and you may be the only one that can make a difference in that person's decision.

Morning came. It was my wedding day, March 9, 2003. I had never walked down an aisle before. My Dad would not give me away (clue), so my stepfather agreed to walk me down the aisle. Instead of the traditional wedding march for my wedding song,

I chose Be Be Winans' "Seeing for the Very First Time," which was ironic since I was as spiritually blind as a bat. Everyone was crying as I came down the aisle, but I don't think they were tears of joy. My daughters looked upset...and rightfully so. Derrick and I said our vows, and we were pronounced man and wife. I kissed my husband, and Prophetess said to me, "Good luck! You're going to need it," as she closed her Bible and walked away, laughing.

Derrick had told me the night before our wedding that he did not want a long reception because of obvious reasons why a man wouldn't, so I agreed to hurry the process along. I guess that's why I was shocked by the fact that he was patiently standing around, talking to everyone. In the meantime, I was a nervous wreck running around, trying to hurry and get all the loose ends tied up so we could leave for our honeymoon. I had never had a honeymoon either. Why was he stalling? Wasn't this the same man that had tried to rip my clothes off the night before? I thought he was in a hurry to get to the hotel.

We stayed around the church for about two hours. I finally had to drag him away from the church by saying, "Let's go, Honey."

On the way to the hotel, he was very quiet, and I began to feel very nervous. It was as though I was seeing for the very first time. The scales were falling off my eyes. As I look back, it is so clear to me what the Devil had done. He had tricked me, and then he allowed me to see the deception after it was too late, just so I would feel hopelessly ashamed.

When we finally were in our room, I thought it would be like the movies or he would at least have the same passion for me that he had had the night before. We both took showers, but his was particularly long. We got in the bed, and he did something I had never thought would happen when a couple was about to consummate their marriage. He turned on the T.V. and started watching basketball.

"What?" I thought to myself. "What is wrong with this man? Is this the same man who begged me to sleep with him when we weren't married, and now that we are, he's doesn't want me anymore?"

My heart sank because at that very moment I knew I had made a big mistake. We watched television for about an hour and finally consummated our marriage. It took all of five minutes! Yes, five minutes! Then, he rolled over and went to sleep. If you do not know by now, the Devil is a trip! And if you're not careful, he will take you on a long one and leave you stranded without a bus ticket home.

I sat on the bed looking crazy until about three o'clock in the morning. I guess that was when I realized he was not waking up to be with me and the honeymoon was over. When I woke up the next morning, he was already up, dressed, and ready to go out and about. I was too afraid to ask him why he did not want to stay in bed with me. Fear came over me because I had to come face-to-face with the truth, that I had made an awful

mistake. He had tricked me, and I knew it, but I was afraid to confront him. He had become the controller, and my reign of power over my decisions was now over.

He did not make love to me anymore on our honeymoon. I tried to hint around, but he would say, "Stop pressuring me!"

I exclaimed to myself, "Oh, my goodness! What? All the time you were pushing me to sleep with you, and now I'm pressuring you!" I was so angry with him, the Devil, and even more with myself. The Devil had not wasted any time letting me know I had married one of his followers.

A week passed, and we were now home, but not much had changed in the libido department. I finally couldn't take it any longer, so I asked him, "Why did you always want to have sex with me before we were married, and now that we are married, you don't want to anymore?"

He replied, "That was then. This is now." That was all the explanation I received, and if I pressed the issue, he would become hostile towards me.

Two weeks passed, and he was becoming more and more hostile toward me. I cried everyday, and that made him even more irritated with me. He would ask me, "What's wrong?"

My only reply was, "Nothing." If I told him the truth, there would be a fight.

Two weeks later, we had planned a trip to Atlanta to go to a wedding. I was excited about going because I was going to get a chance to meet the rest of his family. Mom and the girls rode with us, and his sisters and their children followed along behind us in their car. The traffic was terrible on the ride down. We were stuck in traffic on the highway for three hours, it was ninety degrees outside, and everyone was beyond hot and tired.

Derrick was especially irritated. He got out of the car and turned into a crazy man. He began ranting, raving, and cursing at the traffic. He walked back to his sister's car and started cursing her, too. She got out of the car and began yelling and cursing him back. I was so embarrassed for my children and my mom. I didn't think that Derrick would have ever behaved like that in front of my mother. He honestly did not care, and I became even more frighten of him.

When we finally got to Atlanta, I met his family. I couldn't believe how nice they were and how "well off" they were. It's not that I thought they had no money. It was that Derrick had acted so crazy that I though, well, maybe the rest of the family acted like he did. They kept asking me, "What is a nice girl like you doing with Derrick?"

When I inquired, "What do you mean?" they just laughed and changed the subject. Meanwhile, Derrick left me alone, and I couldn't find him, so I decided to go to our room and get ready for bed. He called the room, accused me of not wanting to be with him, and asked me where I had been. My nerves were a mess as a result of the family's inquires and Derrick's games. He was drunk. Drunk? Wasn't he supposed to be saved? O.K, he did "cuss out" strangers and family on the highway. But drinking! This was too much! I had already been down that road, but that is another whole book. I screamed to myself, "This is a nightmare!"

I would not allow him to stay in my room that night, nor did he want to be there. The following day was the wedding. We were late because he had drunk all night and was tired. It was a beautiful wedding that had cost thousands of dollars, unlike my nightmare of a wedding a couple weeks earlier. It's amazing how God will show you things even in the midst of your storm. I could clearly see that the difference between their wedding – the way they had met, the way the groom treated his bride, and the way he spoke about her at the reception – and my three-week marriage was like night and day. I wanted what they had, not what I had. They had waited; they were engaged for a year; they had a plan; they both were college graduates. He had bought her a house, and she knew he was saved because his fruit matched his life. Derrick knew it too. He was embarrassed by the way he had carried on during the previous weeks and even the night before, but that did not stop him from being mean and out of control even at the wedding. We had planned to leave the next morning to return to Indiana, but I had plans of my own.

When we arrived back to the hotel, I immediately began packing my clothes. Derrick didn't notice because he disappeared as usual. I told the kids and my mother, "Pack as fast as you can! We are out of here!"

Yes, I left my husband in Georgia. He could ride back with his sisters, but he was not riding in my car. He did not return home until the following day. We didn't speak for two days; he stayed next door at his sister's house, an act for which I was eternally grateful. Two days later, he came in the house and said, "I can't believe you left me in Georgia!"

I snapped, "You deserved it!" We kissed and made up, but the damage was done, and I was planning my escape from this man.

Over the next couple of months, we fought every other day. My girls and I were walking on eggshells in our own home. I can't really say what would set him off. He was an abuser, and depending on his mood, he was usually nice toward others but mean and rude to me. He would leave for hours and not tell me where he was going, but when I went some place, he felt as though he needed to be in the car with me. If he wasn't, he would call my cell phone and yell at me all the way home and accuse me of cheating on him.

Derrick became aggressively worse as time went on. I would just pray and try not to trigger his bad moods as much as possible. One particular Sunday, I was getting ready for church when Derrick started in on me with his daily harassment, trying to get me not to go to church. I was just about dressed; I just needed to slip my dress on. He began to grab on me and pushed me onto the bed. He held me down against my will and began raping me. At first, I fought him, but I did not want to alarm my girls, so I calmed myself down and quietly surrendered.

When he had finished, I suppose he felt he had won and that I would stay home and cry. I quietly got up, showered again, put my church clothes on, and went to church. This behavior explained a lot of things to me. The fact was that he used sex as a means of control. Remember he would not sleep with me any other time. What was so ironic was that I had married him because he was pressuring me to have sex with him.

Isn't it amazing how easy it is to become a victim of your own crime? As I look back at that time in my life, I wonder what I could have done differently. My relationship with Jesus was based on finding a husband so that I would not feel hurt or have this desperate hole in my heart. Now, here I was feeling the same hurt, only it was worse because I added physical and mental abuse to my already aching heart. My feeling towards God at this time was anger. I had the nerve to ask God, "Why didn't you stop me from marrying this man?"

It seems that God is sometimes so far removed from our situation. He was so quiet, and I was so hurt and angry. Meantime, Derrick finally got a job. He worked second shift at a meat-packing factory in Logansport, IN. He would often come home extra late, but I was not supposed to question him.

At this time, we had only been married for two and one half months. (All the things that had transpired had all happened in a relatively short amount of time.) I felt like a boxer who had gotten in the ring with no gloves on, to fight against the Devil; the second the bell rang, and he came out swinging. I had been beaten beyond recognition in the first thirty seconds. I was trying to crawl out of the ring, but the Devil kept pulling me back in. This reminds me of what I once heard a famous preacher say, "How do you fight the Devil when you know you can't win? You don't get in the ring with him."

Besides Prophetess, my mother was the only one who really knew about the abuse. Prophetess would mostly take Derrick's side behind my back, that is, until I confronted her. Then she just blatantly told me to my face that she chose to believe Derrick over me, even though she knew he had hit me and raped me.

I felt as if I was in a twilight zone. What was wrong with these people? I felt so hurt and betrayed. Derrick had been going to see Prophetess behind my back and lying to her about everything. Wasn't she a prophet? What happened to all that spiritual discernment she had claimed she had? That was why I was so angry with God. Why hadn't He warned me about her?

He had, but I could not hear Him clearly, because my heart was set on escaping the pain of my situation. Prophetess had made herself the spokesperson for God instead of pointing me to God. I had hung onto her every word because I wanted to know what God was doing before He did it. I did not want to go through the pain of trusting God. Yes, the pain! I had trusted Prophetess, not God, and she had betrayed me! I had chosen to continue to let the world beat me up rather than to submit to the plans of God with no questions asked. I felt God took too long, and He was too vague. I never knew what He was up to! I wanted to be in control. The funny part was now my whole life was totally out of control, and I was outraged.

My mother kept questioning me, "Lori, what are you going to do? I hate to see you go through this," because she knew I had been down this road before. (Again, that is another whole book!)

I told her, "Don't worry, Mom. It will not be long. You know how I am."

The following week Derrick failed to come home. He gave me his excuses, and I did not argue with him. The next day, I went to the courthouse and talked to the clerk about how to file for a divorce. She explained that if there were no children or properties involved, I could just fill out the papers, pay the filing fee, and wait sixty days. The judge would hear our case, and the marriage would be dissolved.

This was music to my ears. I took the papers home that day and began filling them out. After filling out only two of the six pages, I stopped. I decided I should wait until I was absolutely sure this was what I was going to do because I didn't like backtracking. I wanted God to totally convince me that I had no other options. Even though I was upset at Him, I was not completely crazy. I still prayed.

God was silently giving me strength to walk away from this madness. He is so faithful, even when we are just plain stupid. I decided to give Derrick a little hint of what was going on. When he asked to borrow my car, I said, "Yes," knowing that the divorce papers were lying on the front passenger's seat. I left them there to see if he would notice. He didn't.

That weekend was Mother's Day. My thoughts were to give Derrick three strikes, and then, he was out: He had already used two of the three. By now, I had completely filled out the divorce papers, but I had not filed them yet. Saturday night Derrick claimed he had to go to work, and he left. When I woke up on

Mother's Day, he still had not come home, so I waited all day for him. He finally arrived around five o'clock that evening.

I asked, "Where were you?"

He explained that he had been drinking and fell asleep at a friend's house. I reminded him this was the third time this had happened in the past two weeks and although I had put up with a lot of things, I refused to worry about where my husband was every other night. I told him to take his things and please leave my house. To my surprise, he was unusually agreeable. I told him I was filing for a divorce after being married for only two and one half months.

After this, Derrick would come over to the house for the dumbest reasons. Of course, now he was a perfect gentleman, and he was so helpful. The court date of our hearing came quickly, but not soon enough for me.

On the day of the court hearing, I told him to meet me there. He was late, of course, and was inappropriately dressed. He came in, sat next to me, and put his arm around me. I was so embarrassed! He acted as though he did not understand that this was divorce court. The judge asked us a few simple questions, banged the gavel, and made all my bad dreams disappear...so I thought.

On the way out, Derrick put his arm around me, and I shook it off. The judge asked if we would like to be remarried in his chambers. That was one of the few times I really had to bite my tongue to keep from saying two bad words.

Derrick, who had been using my van to haul his tools for his part-time construction job, had driven it to court that day. When I returned home, I asked him to please return my keys and to park the van in the driveway. This should not have presented a problem since he lived next door.

After about an hour had gone by and Derrick still had not returned my van, I decided to drive around the base neighborhood to look for him. I found him sitting on the porch with a woman, so I got out of my car and asked what he was doing.

He said, "Don't worry about it. Just go home."

I got back in my car and drove home. I parked the car, jumped on my daughter's scooter, and rode back around to the house where he was. I dismantled the scooter, placed it in the van, and began throwing Derrick's tools in the street. I was so mad at him.

He jumped off the porch and tried to stop me, but I kept throwing things so fast he could not get to me. Finally, when I had finished cleaning out the back of my van, he grabbed my arm. By this time, we had an audience. You know how everyone loves drama!

I yelled, "Hit me! I dare you!" He balled up his fist, but he could not strike me. There were too many witnesses.

I yelled to his girlfriend, "He's all yours!" went home, and cried.

I later found out that he had been dating her not only before we got married, but also while we were married. Because he lived next door, it was very difficult for me to deal with him and her. Now that their relationship was no longer a secret, they would be outside of my bedroom window talking and hanging out, torturing me.

I asked myself why their relationship hurt me so much when I was the one who had divorced him. I guess the combination of the abuse, the cheating, and the fact that he lived next door to me had compounded the pain.

This went on for about two months. Finally, I could not take it anymore. My plan was to drive to Carmel, IN, and find a place to live. I called Shawn, my ex-husband, and asked him how he felt about the girls and me moving there.

He said he did not mind. God blessed me to find a nice apartment ten minutes away from their dad. It did not take me long at all to move. I didn't tell Derrick I was going to move, and I never saw him until the day I moved out. He came over and inquired, "Where are you moving to?" I told him outside of Indianapolis.

He said, "I never thought you would ever divorce me."

I paused, looked at him, and asked, "What did you expect me to do?"

He replied, "I thought we would eventually get back together."

"For what?" I snapped.

"I don't know," he replied. Then he laughed. He told me that he missed me and that he was so sorry for the way he had treated me. I told him, "I forgive you," and hugged him.

I got in my car, waved goodbye, and drove away from my past. I never saw Derrick again. We were divorced on June 17, 2003, the exact same date that Shawn had filed for divorce one year earlier.

PART THREE: SHIPWRECKED

Chapter Six

There are so many similarities between natural storms, and the two major storms of life I had been through in the course of one year. My ship had finally rested on the island called Carmel, IN. Carmel was paradise compared to the place from which I had moved. There was a Starbucks was on every corner. Wonderful shops to browse through and of course, Carmel High School. The girls were just starting middle school, but I had decided they were going to graduate from CHS one way or another.

Adjustment from Peru to Carmel was fairly easy. The girls were mad at me for moving them away from their friends, but happy to be close to their dad. My divorce had been very hard on me. It was a dysfunctional hurt. I was like an alcoholic having to walk away from alcohol. The victim is clearly aware of the negative effects of this addiction, but still craves it. I believe that is why so many women and men stay in dysfunctional situations.

It is hard work to break the cycle of abuse; withdrawal really hurts, whether it is from drug addiction or from mental or physical abuse.

The reason I chose "Shipwrecked" as the title of this part of my book is pretty much self- explanatory, but I will say that I felt as though I had finally landed on a new island. It did not matter what dangers lay ahead, and believe me, there were dangers. I was just so glad to be away from Derrick and Prophetess. I was ready to start my new life. My walk with Christ at this time was unstable; the things that had transpired in my past confused me. I still didn't get it; I had tried to do the right thing and look what had happened! I knew I had broken a few rules like being unequally yoked, but did I deserve that much punishment? This was my state of mind.

My salvation was strong for a season, and then I became discouraged as well as lonely. I entertained the idea of just being friends with unsaved men, you know, just to have someone with whom to talk, but every time I did, I would become emotionally attached and always put God last. I would rationalize every single relationship, even though I knew in my spirit that God was saying, "Leave him alone."

I decided that I needed something to do besides going to church and taking care of home and the girls, so I decided to go back to school. I was so excited about starting class, but my first few weeks were very frustrating. I thanked God for my kids who knew more in the seventh grade than I did in college. College would have been good for me if I had not been so distracted by life. I had gone to school to fill a void, not to get an education. I was so restless that I could not sit still for very long. I did not want to deal with "me." I was in such a lonely place; I was so miserable.

Since it had become obvious that God was not budging one bit, I decided that I would do things my way. I realize that I use the word "decided" a lot. The reason being, that life is a series of decisions, and each would take me a little bit closer to my place of destination in God…or a little bit further away from the destiny God had for me. In the book of Genesis, the children of Israel were a perfect example of this. A bad decision of choosing to disobey God caused them to take forty years to make a journey that would normally have taken no more than eleven days. (Numbers 14:34)

God has all of eternity, but we have but a short time to make a difference on this side of life. We have the right of free choice, but consequences come with those choices. Wrong decisions that are made knowingly as well as by mistake still carry a price tag. The more we charge on the credit card of life, the more we will have to pay back. Sometimes, we forget how much money we have spent, that is, until we get the bill.

Then we wonder how we could have spent that much.

I was in that place. I felt as if I was in credit card counseling, and I was tired of paying on a balance that was not going down. It was taking too long to pay the debt, and I wanted to shop some more. I told myself that it was too hard to just sit home and do nothing. I felt God did not want me to just waste away doing nothing. And He didn't, but what I didn't understand, nor could I conceive, was the plan that He had for my life. I had thought I trusted God, and I ended up with Derrick! There is so much to be said behind this simple statement: "Lord, I trust you." Now, I am not negating the fact that God died for our sins and that His blood covered our sins completely. For example, if someone robs a bank and afterwards confesses to the robbery, God will completely forgive that person, but he or she will still have to go to prison and reap the consequences of his or her actions. It is the same with God. When we step out of His will, we cease to be under the umbrella of protection. God is always watching and wants to protect us, but He will not force us to obey Him; instead, He will just step back and let the Devil take a few shots at us just so we can learn the difference between the advantages of obedience verses the penalty of disobedience. The choice is always ours, but it may take months or even years for us to fully comprehend this. I pray that by reading my testimony, you can skip that extra trip around the mountain and the tears that go along with it.

Micah

The first time I saw him, I was walking in the factory where I worked. As I previously stated several times before, I worked third shift. At the plant entrance gate, were stairs where Micah would stand and stare at me as I came into the plant for my shift. These steps led down to an area where employees would all gather to watch the clock count down the time before we clocked out. After a month or so, Micah finally got up enough nerve to come find me at my job. He was the type of man who was very hard to read. He would not say outright that he liked me, but he would come and see me every day. Because he would bring me lots of gum, I started to think I had bad breath.

Thankfully, I soon discovered he was addicted to teeth whitening gum, and he loved to share it.

Micah was very kind and generous. I knew better than to date an unsaved man, so I began to question his salvation. I asked him all kinds of questions about church and soon discovered that he knew a lot about the Bible. However, he was holding something back from me. He always wanted to know all of my personal business, but was very private about his.

Micah was a very good-looking man. He had creamy brown skin and soft, curly, dark hair. He was between 5' 11" and 6' and had the biggest brown eyes. As I already stated, he was addicted to teeth whitening gum. His teeth were so white they were almost pale blue. I loved his white smile. We began to talk for hours on the phone about his family and my past. Some men have a way of opening up to a woman that makes her melt; in my case: the sadder a man's childhood, the more attracted I was to him.

For some reason, we women want to show men that we can make it all better, even though we ourselves are messed up, damaged, and hurting. We are sometimes willing to risk our salvation, our pride, and our own mental health to help a depressing-story-telling man.

I was no different. My guard was up, but my window was down halfway. All the Devil really needs is a crack.

About a month went by, and Micah had not yet asked me out. I took this as a good sign because he was not being pushy like Derrick had been. Finally, the time came for Micah to ask me out. Although I was excited about the date, my spirit was a bit uneasy. I kept getting the feeling that this was too good to be true; nevertheless, I continued to ignore God…as always.

I know that sounds harsh, but let's be real for a moment. How many times has God spoken to your heart about something and you rationalized the situation? An example would be asking for spiritual advice from your best "struggling-to-be-saved girlfriend" – you know, the one who always agrees with you when you are sinning and tells you God understands if you're not perfect. Well, that was my way of ignoring God.

Micah pulled up in a sage green baby Lincoln. The car was so beautiful. It had white leather seats. He told me that he was going to take me on two dates. On the first date, he took me horseback riding. We had a really good time. I thought that his choice was very original. He then took me home and told me he would be back later on that evening to take me on our second date.

He returned later on that evening as promised and treated me like a queen. We went to a Japanese steak house where he asked me if he could order for me.

I said, "Yes, of course."

Therefore, he ordered filet mignon with lobster for the both of us. This was the first time I had ever been on a date wherein a man had spent that much money on me in one day. I was totally smitten.

The Devil can be so clever. He knew I wasn't going to be tricked by a broke man, especially after Derrick, who, by the way, never paid one bill while we were married. Micah was like a breath of fresh air. After dinner, we talked for a while, and he took me home. He was a perfect gentleman; still he was a bit distant.

The next few weeks were nice; I invited him to a family dinner with my parents and siblings. He met me at the restaurant where my family and I were eating. He looked quite nervous, so I made sure that I gave him special attention to help his poor nerves. My family, especially my brother Evan, thought he was a little peculiar, but nice.

After that, we started to grow very close. I spent time with him at his house, and he, at mine. One day, I waited to hear from him, but he just did not call. Days turned into one week; weeks soon turned into a month, and still no Micah. My feelings were so hurt, but I was determined that I was not going to contact him unless he called me first. We were not in a relationship, so he owed me nothing, but I thought we were at least friends.

One day, I was at work when a friend of mine named Anthony came to me and asked if Micah and I were dating. I told him that we had been out several times, but I had not talked to him in little over a month. He replied that he had heard Micah was engaged to a woman in Mississippi. My heart sank. There it was again, the feeling of stupidity; it had reared its ugly head once more.

Anthony

Boy, was this a big setup! I had been thrown into the boxing ring with the Devil once again and didn't even know it. The bell had rung, and it was round three. About two weeks later, I found a letter from Anthony in my toolbox. He told me that he had admired me from afar for quite some time and asked if I would go out with him. I put the answer to his letter in his toolbox. I told him "no" and that I had had enough of lying men to last me a while. He continued to write me every day for a while. Each time, I would reply, "I don't trust you, nor do I want to be in a relationship."

I need to let you know that the Devil is very patient; he, too, has eternity, but he knows that his end is damnation. He wants to date you so he can take you to Hell with him. Furthermore, he does not care how long it takes, because he knows how to court a woman: The adversary is not always broke or a rough neck; sometimes he can be quiet-natured, have a kind smile, and have a good-paying job.

Now, I am not referring to all men as evil, but I can unequivocally say that whatever your weakness is, the Devil will bait you with it. Mine was unsaved men, and I feel sure that Christian men would say the same about unsaved women.

Now, I know what you are thinking, "I'm not like that!"

Well, neither was I, but when I stopped listening to God, there was only one other voice left, and that was my flesh. Walking in the flesh is sin. (Romans 8:3) The wages of sin is death, and the Devil's job is to cause both you and me to sin by any means necessary.

There are two kinds of people in the spiritual world: believers and unbelievers. I knew that the Bible said, "*Be not unequally yoked with unbelievers,*" (2 Corinthians 6:14) but I always found myself going down that road…unintentionally, of course. I always put up a good fight in the beginning, but for some reason, it was hard for me to cut the relationship completely off. I did not want to come off as being mean or a little over the top, so I stayed friends with these men. I did not want to hurt their feelings, even if I was hurting God's by being disobedient.

I continued to receive letters from Anthony every night, and, of course, I always replied to those letters. It was fun, sort of like being in high school. No one ever wrote letters anymore, and I was attracted to the idea of someone taking the time to hand write me a letter. Most of his letters were four or five pages long. They were full of compliments and questions about who I was and what I believed. The letter writing seemed so innocent at the time, but looking back on the situation, I was once again a casualty of Satan's battle tactics. That is why I am sharing each of my experiences in detail.

After sometime of playing the cat and mouse game, Anthony came by my job. He brought me a rose and said he just wanted to see me before he left to go down South for a motorcycle race. Had I mentioned he rode a motorcycle? Well, ladies, need I say more? As I said, "he," meaning the Devil, knows what we like.

When he got back, I gave in and went out with him, but I was still going to church and reading my Word that is, after reading Anthony's letters first, and answering him back. I was no longer worshiping before God. I felt too guilty to do that; besides, I did not want to hear God say, "Leave him alone."

I was back to using Satan's credit card once more, adding up more charges than I was willing to pay. Word of my dating Anthony got back to Micah somehow, and he was distraught. I had not heard from him for days on end, but he was acting as though I had betrayed him. When I confronted him about being engaged, he said that it was true, but he did not love his fiancé. He loved me. I was speechless, not because I had nothing to say, but because I was trying to not hurt his feelings. Yes, I know how stupid that sounds, but it was the truth.

When he finished crying and giving me all his excuses, I told him, "I'm sorry, Micah. I'm seeing Anthony now. There is nothing I can do to help you. Goodbye." I felt really sad and glad at the same time, glad because Micah had gotten what I felt he deserved and sad because I knew my relationship with him had been unequally yoked. I was feeling just as guilty toward God as Micah was feeling toward me for having deceived me.

Micah continued to try and contact me, but I would just ignore his calls. By now, Anthony and I were becoming really good friends. He was very patient with me. He was quiet and soft-spoken; I liked that quality in him. He took me shopping a lot and always made sure I had money. This approach was different from what I was accustomed. I was still going to school at this time, but I do not know how, with my busy lifestyle of the rich and famous.

The girls spent a lot of time with their Dad because he lived right down the street. They had a key to his apartment and would often ride the school bus to his home and let themselves in. This meant that I had too much free time on my hands. I should have been studying, but it was hard for me to do the right thing in other areas of my life when I was doing wrong in my spiritual life. That was the way God had wired me to be. I was useless without Jesus Christ, so I quit school.

I continued to date Anthony and invited him to church. After he had gone to church with me, he started calling the church people hypocrites, accusing them of being in the club the night before. What could I say? Not everybody who went to church was saved, and I wasn't any better. In addition, Anthony himself had just recently divorced, so he was in no condition for a new relationship. I told him this repeatedly, but he insisted that he was fine.

One day, he asked me if I wanted to go with him to look for a house, and I said, "Yes, are you moving?" He replied, "I was thinking about moving to Carmel in the future, and I want to buy a house that you can live in until I move to Carmel."

I questioned his motives because I had learned from my experience that there was always a catch. I repeatedly told him I was not going to live with him.

He agreed and proceeded to let me pick out our house. We looked for several months and finally settled on a nice four-bedroom tri-level. The house was very nice and had a beautiful fireplace that was set in a stone wall and stretched across the entire wall. The backyard had a large apple tree, and the neighbors' yards were completely fenced in all around us, so there was no need to put up our own fence. I was excited about getting a house because it was what I was accustomed to living in during the nine years when Shawn and I were married. The only major difference was the lush neighborhood that accompanied this wonderful house.

Anthony had not once mentioned marriage, and I thought to myself, "He is crazy if he thinks I will live with him without being married!" The time finally came to sign the mortgage papers. I was there with him, and he actually put my name on the title to the house without putting my name on the mortgage. I thought that was fine with me. He also agreed to pay half of the mortgage and expenses. He kept his word and allowed me to move in…alone. This was a bitter-sweet move because my spirit would not allow me to find peace in my soul. I knew my living in this beautiful neighborhood was not going to last. Two months later, Anthony slowly but surely started moving his things in. I continued to warn him, "I will not live with you!"

He told me that he would take the downstairs bedroom for the sake of the kids. He worked second shift, so it would be as if he were not ever there when the girls were home. Anthony and I rarely ever spent time together after he moved in because I still worked midnights. It seemed that we lived two separate lives like roommates. I hated this because I knew that it was wrong. In fact, he wasn't fun anymore, so I gave him until Christmas to see if he was going to propose to me. After all, I had already told him I would not live in sin, but I didn't think he had taken my threats seriously.

Christmas Day came, and he gave me a little gray box. Of course, I was excited, until I opened the box and saw diamond earrings. After stewing over my major disappointment, I decided to confront him with my dissatisfaction. I asked him if he thought we would ever get married. He said, no, and added that he did not love me although he cared a great deal for me.

The next few weeks, I searched for an apartment. Once I found my place, I sat down and told him, "I can't do this anymore." He disagreed with me and said, "How do you know if you're compatible with a person unless you live with them first?" I answered, "I don't know, but God is holding me accountable for my actions." I told him I should never have gotten involved with someone who wasn't saved anyway.

Ironically, he didn't seem to be that upset with me and kept reminding me I could stay as long as I wanted. He just didn't get it, nor did he want to understand it, but it was not my job to convert a sinner to a saint. That is why God had said in II Corinthians 6:14, "*Be not unequally yoked with unbelievers....*" I don't know why I had chosen to go around that mountain again. I believe that we as women get tired of waiting on God, and we compromise, not understanding that it is more painful to open our heart to an unsaved man, only to have the wages of sin demand payment of our crime before we get to the checkout counter. Apparently, I had thought I was the exception to the rule or that this special rule did not apply to me because I had already been through so much!

It was getting close to February, and I planned to be in my apartment very soon. I had emotionally detached myself from Anthony. Deep down in my heart, I had known all along that this living arrangement was not going to work out because, as I said before, "God doesn't bless mess!" He never goes along with our plans. It's all about obedience to Him. Yes, I know it's hard to get the hang of it, but after going around the mountain so many times, it should become easier to obey. I just liked the challenge of the mountain, I guess. I didn't really believe that God was as immovable, when it came to my disobedience. I was still in a process that had now taken over three and one half years of my life, and I still had not caught on! **Hint: God will never compromise His standards because we can't help what we do.** If we do decide to do things our own way, we should make sure that we have plenty of manna because it is going to be an extra long trip around that mountain.

Well, I was angry with Anthony, and I was sure he couldn't care less. I think I was angrier with myself, but I did not want to feel guilty, so it was easier to channel my anger toward him. For Valentine's Day, my good friend Neasha invited me to a singles' party the church was having. I said "no" but after thinking about my situation, I decided, "Yes, I'm going to that party. It will make me feel better." So we went. It was nice; everyone except Neasha and me was so tense. We were goofing off because we weren't really expecting to meet anyone. We had been to all the singles' meetings that the surrounding churches have had. There were always lots of women – some in their late forties and many in their fifties as well – and two men – one old and one five feet tall.

Now, I wasn't dogging out these vertically challenged brothers. They were some of the nicest men, and they would treat us single women like the queens we aspired to be, but let's face it! I was 5'7" and I had some meat on my bones. It was hard to imagine myself with a little man, and so I didn't take the party very seriously. Well, by the end of the night, I was standing at the far end of the table, near a man that seemed to be very shy and out of place. I said, "Hello, are you O.K.?"

He quietly replied, "Yes."

I asked, "Why are you sitting down here by yourself?"

When he replied, "I'm kind of shy," I introduced myself, and we talked for a bit longer. I then went back to my seat and talked with Neasha. I didn't say anything else to this man for the rest of the evening. However, when we were praying at dismissal and everyone was told to hold hands, I ended up holding hands with this him. While we were praying, he was rubbing my hand with his thumb as a parent reassures a child when the child is anxious. After prayer, he asked me for my number. I didn't want to give him my cell phone number, so I asked him for his number. He asked me to call him that night. When Neasha and I got in the car, she asked me who he was. I told her that his name was Craig, and "I think he was rubbing my hand with his thumb during prayer."

Craig

I didn't call him that night, but waited until the following evening. However, he had mentioned he worked midnights, too, so I decided to wait until I got to work to call. When I finally did call, he asked why I had not called him the night we met.

I told him that it was late when I got home, so I had gone to bed. He seemed a little upset with me because I had not called that night, so I apologized and continued our conversation. A couple of days went by, and I was trying to avoid Craig because I was trying to get my things out of Anthony's house as soon as possible. I was ashamed that I had even lived with Anthony.

Craig, on the other hand, was saved, and…he had been raised like me in a Christian home. So I quickly moved and stored the rest of my things in Anthony's garage. I made one fatal mistake; I called Craig from Anthony's house phone. He had no idea that I had just moved into my own place, so he assumed that Anthony's number was my home phone number.

That day he called me back on Anthony's house phone, and I answered. He asked me if I would like to meet him for coffee at Starbucks.

I thought to myself, "Wow! What a blessing. I met this nice man, and so soon after leaving Anthony's house." **Hint: Uh, we need to chill until we hear God's voice telling us to proceed.** Going from one relationship into another takes our focus off God because we never stop long enough to hear anything He has to say.

I really wasn't sure how serious Craig was, but because of my past relationships, I was sort of guarded. It had not dawned on me what I was doing when I called him from Anthony's, and now he had Anthony's house phone number! So I did the only thing I could: I called him and came clean. I told him the whole dreadful story. He began to question why I had been at the singles' party that night; I told him I didn't actually think that I would meet anyone there.

Well, he decided he wanted to see me in spite of my bad choices. We talked for about a week on the phone before we actually met at Starbucks. I was excited about meeting him and looked forward to starting over yet again. I prayed on the way over and asked God to forgive me for my past. I prayed that Craig would be all that he claimed to be as a Christian. When I entered Starbucks, the air was filled with chatty voices and the sound of a small band. The band was playing Jazz; the atmosphere was nice. That was one of the reasons why I liked Starbucks so much.

Craig and I talked for what seemed like hours. I loved the fact that he had been raised in a sanctified home like me. He told me that he was divorced and had not been in a relationship since the divorce three years ago. He had not been with another woman since his wife.

I wondered why he had not been in any relationships, but then again I thought maybe he was waiting for me. At the end of the night, Craig walked me to my car and held both my hands. He leaned down and lightly touched my lips with his. His kiss was soft and gentle and did not feel the least bit intrusive. As I got in my car, I was on cloud nine. I smiled all the way home. That night, I sent up a thank you to God and thought to myself that he could be the one.

Over the next several weeks, Craig and I were constantly on the phone. He had two sons that he had full custody of. They were about the same ages as my girls. After about a month or so, we let the kids meet, they were crazy about each other. It was like the Brady bunch minus two people. His father lived with him, too. Craig's dad was very nice; he cooked and cleaned for Craig and the boys. Everyone got along beautifully except there was one problem: Craig was extremely jealous. Since he knew that Anthony worked at Chrysler, too, he would continually ask me if I had seen or talked to him at work. Most days I told him "no," and it was true.

I never lied to Craig because I didn't want to mess up my relationship with him. Isn't it ironic that we can treat our relationship with God as if it were casual; and as soon as a man comes along, we decide we are going to do everything within our power to be real and true to that person? Wow, I had some nerve!

Things seemed to be going very well for Craig and me. He took me on the best dates; we would talk on the phone for hours or go to the park and just sit and talk. We shared our dreams and what we wanted for our kids. We agreed that they would all go to college no matter what it cost, and we agreed that we would trust God in our relationship and not let sin destroy us.

One day, while I was at his place and his dad and I were cooking, he came in the kitchen and whispered in my ear, "I think I'm falling in love with you." I looked up at him, and he smiled at me and walked out of the kitchen. This was the first time since my divorce that a man had told me that without a lot of drama and no strings attached. I had not sinned, and it felt wonderful! I thought to myself, "Finally, God, he is the one!"

Craig and I spent a lot of time in prayer, but it was becoming more and more difficult to be around each other and not be physically attracted to each other. We went to Bible study and to church on a regular basis. We went to church functions together, along with the kids. As our relationship progressed, we became frustrated because we knew that we had only been together a little over three months, but because we were fighting our flesh, it seemed like an eternity! We were talking one day about our frustrations, and he asked me what I thought about marriage. I told him the last time I got married, I had rushed into it, and it did not turn out very well.

So he asked, "Lori, what are we going to do?"

"I don't know," I told him. Somehow, the idea of being married scared me, but I still loved him very much. There was something very special about this man. He was very intense and very romantic. I felt his love for me was genuine, but we were almost obsessive with each other. My daughters now refer to this closeness as "cult love."

On Good Friday weekend, he bought us tickets to see *The Passion* play. (To this day, I still have the dress I wore to the play.) When Craig came to my house to pick me up, he brought me a corsage. I had never been treated in such a romantic way…well, not since Micah. Micah had been nice, but Craig had my heart. In my mind, Craig was different because he was saved. I didn't feel guilty for going out with him. The date went beautifully. When he took me home, he walked me up to my place and came in. We talked and talked, and then we kissed and kissed and kissed some more. Then we sinned.

The next day, I felt like the air had gone out of our big balloon. He came over, and we prayed and asked God to forgive us. He told me, "I don't think I can do this anymore; I need to meet with your father." I knew why he wanted to meet Dad, but I played dumb. They met, and he asked my Dad if he could marry me. My Dad gave him a hard time, but he eventually told him "yes." Now, that was really the first time a man had ever gone to my father and asked if he could marry me.

After leaving from dinner with my father, Craig was very quiet. He took me to a place called The Wishing Well Park, and we walked along the trail way, holding hands but not really saying much. The park was wooded with a small stream that flowed through it. As we walked onto the bridge that overlooked the stream, Craig stopped, reached in his pocket, and pulled out a white box. He bent down on one knee and asked me to be his wife. I remember embracing the moment. I savored every second of it, and tears filled my eyes as I told him, "Yes, I would love to be your wife!"

Craig placed the beautiful diamond ring on my left hand. The rest of the afternoon, we spent making plans for our future together. We planned on getting premarital counseling and had the books and workbooks that went along with it. Every detail was calculated. We began to look for a place to live, one that would accommodate a family of six. We still were not sure if Craig's father was going to stay with us or not.

We finally found a townhouse that would accommodate us all. The only problem with the place was that Craig's lease was up at the end of May and he needed to move quickly. I suggested that he move into the townhouse and that we wait to get married at a later date. I did not want to get married so quickly, just because it would be the convenient way to solve a problem. I told him to give me some time alone to think about this, but he began to pressure me. He needed to know as soon as possible, and I understood that. Craig felt like he could not afford to live in the townhouse alone, but I felt it was stupid to rush into getting married strictly because of his financial burdens. This was where everything began to shift.

Remember the woman named Prophetess? I do not know what possessed me to call her, but I did. I guess I wanted to find out if I should marry this man. I knew she had, I will loosely say, "gifts of the spirit," but of what spirit was the question. I should have been asking God instead of her. I told her about Craig and our dilemma. She began to tell me he was a controlling man and that he had issues that stemmed from his past and not to marry him.

When I got off the phone with her, I was more confused than ever. All of my premarital bliss was crushed into a big ball of confusion. She still had that effect on me. My thoughts raced back to being married to Derrick and how I had not taken heed to the warning signs. Could God be warning me about this man also? My life was right back to where it used to be: full of confusion, doubt, and fear. I decided to pray and ask God what I should do.

Meantime, Craig was pressuring me for an answer. I finally told him what Prophetess had said about him. He was so angry at her and at me for having called her, but he still could not persuade me to change my mind about waiting. He asked me to give him Prophetess's number so he could speak with her. I told him I did not think it was a good idea because I knew that she would blow him out the water, meaning he could not win an argument with her.

Well, I folded and gave Craig her number. He called her, and they talked for an hour or so. I had no idea what was being said until after he got off the phone. He told me we needed to talk. He began to question me about my past and asked me about things that only Prophetess would know. She was so clever in how she could plant seeds of destruction. I will not give her the credit that belongs to the enemy because "We wrestle not against flesh and blood, but against powers, against the rulers of darkness of this world, against spiritual wickedness in high places." (Ephesians 6:12)

My heart was crushed. How could she be so evil? Prophetess had taken the true things that she knew about me and added lies in order to twist the meaning. The truth mixed with lies is the Devil's main weapon he uses against us. He did it to Eve in the Garden to confuse her, and he will continue to do that until we begin to rightly divide the Word of truth for ourselves. That is why it is important to "Study to show thyself approved unto God, a workman that needed not to be ashamed, rightly dividing the word of truth." (2 Timothy 2:15)

What was I going to do now? I had already put down a deposit on the townhouse even though I was not sure of what I was going to do. Craig began to question our getting married and could not understand why this so-called woman of God would lie on me, especially since I was the one who had called her. I was defenseless against her. After this, he started acting very mean toward me and talking crazy to me. We had one conversation concerning the townhouse and what we were going to do about it, but I had decided regardless of whether we got married or not, I was going to move out of my place, since the neighbors were loud and I could not get any rest.

Because of the pressure brought on by what Prophetess had done, I agreed to marry Craig because I felt I was going to lose him if I didn't. Isn't it crazy how the Devil can so quickly come in like a flood and mess us up? However, we must remember that the Bible says, "And for we know that all things work together for the good of those who love God and are called according to his plan." (Romans 8: 28) I had lost sight of the fact that God was in control and will always be in charge of my life. Nevertheless, it seemed as though it was the Devil who was presently in control, but God had allowed these things to happen. Nothing slips pass His eyes: "The eyes of the Lord are in every place, watching the evil and the good." (Proverbs 15:3)

During the next conversation Craig and I had, he said he did not want to get married anymore. I was devastated; my heart was racing, and I began to cry on the phone. I asked him, "Where am I going to live? I already gave up my apartment!"

He said, "You should have thought about that before you done that!"

I could not believe this was the man that I was about to marry. It was like Derrick's madness all over again. I hung up the phone and cried my eyes out. I began to have the old anxiety attacks that I had had when I was married to Derrick. Then it seemed as if the Lord was saying, "Get a hold of yourself and take care of your business." Therefore, I got up, dried my eyes, and headed over to the apartment complex where I had put the money down on our townhouse.

While I was on my way, my phone rang. It was Craig calling me. I hit the ignore button and kept going. He continued to call me the whole time I was dealing with the lady about the apartment, but I refused to answer my phone. I took the down payment off of the townhouse and put it down on an apartment so that my kids and I would have a place to live. After doing so, I headed over to Craig's apartment to return his ring. I slid the ring under the door and then called him to let him know that the ring was under the door. As I was getting back into my car, he ran down the steps and tried to stop me from leaving. He stood in front of my car and held onto the hood. Of course, I wasn't going to run over him no matter how badly I wanted to; that would be vehicular manslaughter, and I wasn't going to jail because of this man. He was screaming my name, but I would not respond. I put the car in reverse just long enough to clear him so I could go. Craig jumped into his car and followed me for two miles, beeping his horn. I finally pulled over.

I yelled, "Why are you following me? You said that you didn't want to marry me!" "Can we at least talk?" he pleaded.

I answered, "Not here on the side of the road. I'm going home." I got back in my car and drove home. Naturally, he followed me. The girls were not home from school yet. I was glad for that. He came in and began to apologize for his behavior.

I told him I was upset about everything, the way he had talked to me on the phone and the fact that he had believed Prophetess over me. He got down on his knees again, put the ring back on my finger, and said, "I don't want you to ever take this ring off again. I am so sorry, Lori."

I was thinking, "This ring is going to come off in the next five minutes. Watch

and see!" but I said, "Craig, I have something to tell you. I gave up our townhouse and put the money on an apartment for my kids and me."

He was furious! He protested, "I tried to call you over and over!"

I told him I knew, but I was busy talking to the lady about my apartment.

He asked, "What about our place? Where am I going to live?"

I told him he could still get the place. "I just won't be living there with you."

Needless to say, he wasn't a happy camper when he left for home.

Over the next several days, I just couldn't shake all that had transpired in such a short amount of time. Craig gave me the ultimatum that if I did not marry him by the end of May, he didn't want to get married at all.

I told him I would return his ring to him within the next day or so, and I kept my word. After returning the ring, I was so hurt by the whole thing. I felt as if Prophetess had thrown me under the bus that Craig was driving. Craig and I talked a few times, but after a few arguments with him, I hung up on him, and I decided not to take his calls anymore.

This time, I had officially hit rock bottom. I told the Lord I would not date another man or get involved with another relationship until God completely healed me from this man. I would not use another relationship to substitute for or to cover up my pain. I locked myself away from the world of men and completely surrendered to God. I began to only watch TBN and the Word Network. I refused to watch any movies that were romantic. I became a depressed hermit and was very cynical about love and relationships. I grieved over Craig for close to six months and refused to go to any social functions out of fear of running into Craig with another woman. I had gone from the bondage of disobedience into a spirit of fear and depression. At the same time, I prayed and asked the Lord to deal with Craig's mind. The Lord was saying to my spirit, "All things work together for the good," but I hurt so badly!

Chapter Seven

August 25, 2005

God, I thank you for taking me through the winter. I chose green this time to remind me of spring, the season that brings a renewal of faith, trust, love, and commitment. Lord, it has been three and a half months since Craig and I broke up. I thought I would die, and I did over and over again, daily. I wasn't quite ready to write just yet, but I felt the Lord urging me to write. I talked to Craig today. He sounded crazier than ever. Satan has a grip on him, but God has the last say so. I stood up to him once more. He called me a manipulator and said I had to have things my way.

I said, "No, look in the mirror, and you will only see a reflection of yourself. And as far as my way, no, it's God's way or the highway." I feel as though I can see him clearer and clearer; he's pretty jacked up. I will still pray for him, but I cannot be a part of his life.

The Lord spoke to me tonight and said, "I used Craig to heal you, and I will use you to heal him also." I often said I was his blessing. *God is strengthening me. I don't know how? Nevertheless, God's grace is so amazing. I cannot function without him. Lord, I just want to say thank you. Sometimes, I want to complain about my life or how boring it is, but boring is good. Thank you for transforming me into a good mom.*

This was the first time I had written in months. I had been too busy dating and participating in high-speed car chases. I was grateful for having a place to live. My apartment was cute, and I felt like I could finally breathe again. I could now resume my life of solitude and watching TBN (Trinity Broadcasting Network). I felt as if I did not know what else to do with my life. It was as though I was stuck in this miserable place. I was either dating, which would always turn into a disaster, or I was at home… alone, because I was afraid that I would make another mistake and have to pay the ultimate price for it.

Being single can be a very confusing time in life. Our identity changes so many times in our mind as well as in real life. I was ready to become a wife again because that was what was the most comfortable for me. I, like most women that have been married, knew what an exhausting job being a wife and a mother could be, but I enjoyed taking on the challenge. In fact, it was hard for me to think of myself as being good at anything else, neither did I want to be. I felt as if I had invested many years of my life perfecting the art of being a wife and a mother, and I do not think I had a desire to do anything else. I could not envision the possibility of God using me in a profound way. I had once had dreams of being a powerful woman used by God, but I felt that because of all my mistakes, it was too late to redeem the time. Little did I know that my mistakes would be a big part of my testimony and my journey to where God was leading me.

As I was writing in my journal, I knew I was writing for a purpose, but my mind could not imagine the road that was ahead of me and all of the twists and turns I would have to make. It is easier to do what is familiar to us no matter how miserable we are. Well, that is how I felt. God knew that I did not have the strength to see pass my pain. I thought He was looking for perfection, and I could not be perfect. I had tried and tried. I thought the reason I wasn't going anywhere but around in circles was that I kept failing God. He knew I was going to fail before He called me. My view of God was distorted. I thought He was mad at me fifty percent of the time, and the other fifty percent of the time, I was making up for all the wrong it had done. Asking God for forgiveness was not enough for me.

Please don't misunderstand me. Being obedient to God is still very important to Him because there are consequences of sin, although no one is going to live a perfect life in exchange for God's blessings. God wants us to love and obey Him, not just to get a husband or to get out of trouble. These are the reason why we fall short so many times. But if we can learn to just love, trust, and obey God just because it is the right thing to do, we would be on the road to recovery sooner and could move on to the incredible life that He still has planned for our future.

August 30, 2005

To God be the glory! Lord, I thank you for another day. I thank you for your grace and mercy. I thank you for getting me out of the house down to the Fountain Square, my favorite spot. God, I thank you for not letting the Devil sift me as wheat, even when I was willing to let him myself. PMS is funny. It causes you to go through so many ranges of emotions, from being sad, to being super sensitive in a worship service, to crying because you watched a love story on TV. Well, I have experienced all of that this week. Anthony came by my job to spend some time with me, and I had a good time. However, I felt no attraction to him, but then when he mentioned another woman, I went off on him! I really need to stay far away from him. I don't love him, but he has become my security blanket.

It is a very bad habit. It reminds me of when I was younger and used to have what I called a backup boyfriend, and I was, in return, his. However, as you grow older, it is really hard to be honest and saved and not play those childish games.

Anthony has always been in the background, and I don't like it, and Craig wants me to be his security blanket. I hate being 38 years old and having to play the games I did when I was 16 years old. It used to be that men played games around the age of 20 to about 35 years old. Now men are having a 2ⁿᵈ childhood at 40, something I don't want — to have to marry an old man — but most men in their 30's and early 40's are looking out only for themselves! They are as bad as 16-year-old boys are! Then when they are done playing, around 46 or so, they get scared because they know 50 is coming and they need a good woman and want to settle down. But by then, women are mad and bitter from all the games men have played, and they are not taking that stuff anymore. Men are now wondering why women are tripping and have become so mean!

Lord, I am so tired of the games. I'm so glad you're not like man, that you are a constant companion. I heard a tape today about women; everybody has a story, and it goes like this. Women's twenties are spent carelessly and free, leading up to their thirties, which are spent balancing a husband, kids, job and home. Then at the end of their thirties, most women find themselves alone due to their husbands walking out on them. Then there is a time of recovery, and in their forties, they are reborn again. They begin to discover who they really are as well as find love again, and enjoy sex with their husbands a lot more than they ever imagined.

After hearing that, I felt a real sense of comfort. God is trying to lead us into this time in our lives as graciously as possible. He knows I am prone to make major mistakes and that I could forfeit any good thing He has for me. My impatience is sometimes my own worst enemy…and the fact that I feel sorry for myself. I also have the tendency to get depressed. I have to force myself to get out of the house. I love my daughters, and they always check with me to make sure I'm all right, but I feel bad when they leave, so I tend to stay locked up in my room. But I'm learning to get out more, and it does me good. God, thank you for the push! I needed it. Well, I really don't have much wisdom this month. I haven't wanted to write anything negative. I have been through a horrible summer, and I didn't want to write about it; nevertheless, God is still good and faithful. I'm looking forward to a new season.

I was growing spiritually, but I couldn't see it. All of my failures had led up to this moment in my life. Because of my mistakes, I was better able to gain sight of a bigger picture. Before all of this drama had taken place, I had had only one goal in life, to recapture the essence of the former life that I had lost. It had been natural for me to want to be married and have a good job as well as serve God from the pews of the church. I just wanted to be normal like every other woman.

Most women do not want to tip the boat and start over again. I don't think we women realize how hard we really try to keep things together with our children, our homes, our appearance, and especially our relationship with our husband. When the storms of life come crashing in on our little world of perfection, we find out we don't have any power to save anything or anyone, and do you know why? Because we haven't put God first! How could we have the strength to fight the storms of life when the foundation of our home has been built upon sand? The storms of life will continue to come and go, so we must continue to nail down those spiritually vulnerable places in our lives by securing our relationship with God first.

When we were young, let's say in our early twenties, life seemed to hold no threats besides the occasional boyfriend drama and possibly the threat of not finding a mate. As we aged, we found a mate and, in addition to having children, we became more relaxed and began to let down our guards. This is precisely what Satan wanted us to do. We became involved with our kids' soccer games, going to the gym, looking good on Sunday morning, and having a clean home. In the meantime, Satan was working behind the scenes like a termite, eating away at the foundation of our husband and kids, as well as our own stability.

Then came the storm, and suddenly it was all over. It seemed as though we had had no warning. It was not fair that this had happened to our house rather than to our neighbor's house, even though, we felt, our neighbor probably deserved it more than we did. I will further discuss the subject of storms in detail later on in this book.

August 31, 2005

Lord, I thank you for a new day. I thank you for faithfulness even when I feel like crap. I thank you for good daughters that care about me. I thank you for your Word that rocked me to sleep like a baby, and the same Word that allows me the courage to get up and face another day in this awful world we live in. Sometimes, I don't want to be grateful. I want to complain, but, God, you whisper in my ear, "It's going to be fine." You give me hope.

I sometimes feel so stupid about telling anyone my crazy dreams or the things I hear you whisper to me. I don't even like to write them down for fear that I will have to share my journal with others someday, and I know I will, probably with my kids, and they will get to know me not just as Mommy.

Anyways, I talked to my friend Neasha today. We shared some things with each other about loneliness. I really thought I was the only one who was so desperately lonely. It was not that I was happy that she was lonely, too. But I was relieved to know that there are others out there hurting and that I am not dysfunctional. Loneliness is a part of other people's lives, too. I didn't like the fact that she said, "Oh, well, I guess I will get my reward in Heaven; I guess I will just go through the motions of life." What she had said sounded so wickedly familiar to how I felt! That is what had me so devastated about my divorce; I thought I was destined to live out my life as Gina Bail, the only virgin that I knew that was over fifty years old.

When I look at many single women, they seem to be old, all dried up and desperate! I was determined that, that was not going to be me. What these women had become, I don't have to become, and neither does Neasha. They are bound by their circumstances because they don't know anything else. "This is the way it is and will always be." That is what I heard Neasha say, but the Word of God says, "I **know the plans I have for you… plans to prosper you, not to harm you."** *I have to believe the Word over my thoughts…over the words that I hear Satan saying in my ear. No matter how lonely I get or feel, I am coming out of this pit. It is only temporary! God is going to avenge his women, and He will say to me someday, "Woman, your faith has made you whole! Woman, thou are loosed!"*

As I read over my journal, I myself was encouraged…so much so that I wrote in the margin of my journal, "God honors the seeds of faith that we plant. They grow when we least expect it. 3/27/07"

I had not yet accepted the idea of being single. My breakup with Craig had crushed my heart. I was now determined that I would not use another relationship to heal my breakup and that I would allow God to heal my heart. Even though I felt this way, the Devil was trying to drag me back into my old ways. He tortured me with thoughts of being an old maid by reminding me of all the single women that I had seen growing up in my church. I resented the idea of being desperate and hopeless because I had seen those kinds of women my whole life.

What I didn't understand was that God gives us the freedom and the power to become powerful women of God who live full successful lives. I was obsessed with the thought of being married before I turned forty years old. Nevertheless, I had so much to learn about myself that I could not see what God saw, and so I fought with the Devil constantly about my singleness. I thank God because He knew how I felt, and He had such wonderful plans for my life. However, He also knew it would take some time for me to see myself the way He saw me. Change is very painful, but necessary; in order to become all that God has called us to be. Some of the women I had seen as I was growing up all had one thing in common: They had refused to change. Year after year, they sat in the same place, wore the same hairstyle, and complained about the same things, the shortage of saved men in the church. Not one of those women had ever gotten married, and to this day, they are all still single because that is what they chose. Their present situation was not a punishment sent from God.

God was slowly reprogramming my thoughts; I went from believing God to restore my marriage to God's being my Deliverer and my Healer of yet another broken heart. I didn't understand my pain. I just knew that it was real and that I was tired of living in constant agony. I did not know how to make it stop. God was breaking down the layers of damage that had settled on my heart over the years since my youth.

September 6, 2005

To God be the glory for the things He has done! I was re-listening to a tape rental from the library called "Chocolate for the Woman's Soul." It spoke of a lady who was making a decision to date after being divorced three years prior. Her friend suggested that she make a list of the qualities that she desired in a mate, and so she did, and she narrowed it down to fifteen qualities. Her friend then told her she needed to make sure she had the same qualities as well. Well, I got to thinking this is a very good idea, and so I wrote my own list of qualities.

Qualities of My Man List

1) *Loves God more than himself or me*

2) *Loves me as Christ Loves the Church*

3) *Kind, not jealous*

4) *Can love my kids (package deal)*

5) *Good sense of humor*

6) *Loves water and nature*

7) *Loves to travel*

8) *Impulsive, yet not dumb*

9) *Has wisdom, but not bossy*

10) *Knows how to treat his lady*

11) *Romantic*

12) Good lover

13) Patient

14) Knows and loves the Word of God

15) Doesn't mind helping with housework

16) Handy around the house

After writing this list, I realized that it was just as important that I was able to accept these things as a way of life for myself, too, and to understand that I am not always humorous, patient, or anxious to do housework. I was not spontaneous, nor did I feel romantic all the time. Why, then, should I expect someone else to have a perfect track record? The only thing I could really say was that the most important thing was that **the person loved God and that he was willing to receive love and forgiveness from God. Without that, he could not give what he did not have or had not received from God.** *I cannot believe it has taken me so long just to know that! It would have saved me years of heartache and years of asking God why? Why? Why? Well, God, I thank you for the answers through your Word.*

The point is don't get involved with a man who doesn't love God or who hasn't received forgiveness from God because there is a hole in his heart, and he seeks out women to fill only what God can fill. When an unsaved man uses you to fill that hole, it doesn't stay filled. We as women will somehow blame ourselves and think that we were not pretty enough or thin enough or that we didn't do enough for him. That unsaved man, in return, will never admit that he was really the one with the problem; he will make you believe that everything was your entire fault and that everything negative you thought you have had about yourself was true. We women are hurt by this; meanwhile, he moves on to the next woman to temporarily fill the hole in his heart once again or his ego, whatever you want to call it, and we are left picking up the pieces of our shattered hearts again. There is a solution; give God your heart, and trust Him with your cares and concerns. Before you become involved, you must decide if you will listen to what the

Holy Spirit is saying: "Not now!" "Not him!" or another voice saying, "Well, even if he isn't the one, you can still be friends."

You cannot be friends with some people, especially the Devil! Now I'm not implying that ever man is the Devil, but the following rules do apply: If you have just gotten out of a manipulating or sexually sinful relationship, if you're on the path to doing right, and if you as well as that man know that you are fresh out of a sinful relationship – you are not ready for a friendship/relationship. I don't care if he is T.D. Jakes' twin brother! Or even if the relationship was not sinful, there is what we call recovery time! It usually takes at least 6 months or more to recover. If he comes along right after a breakup, don't think that "God is so good!" Wrong! God is good, not stupid! He is not going to put you immediately into another relationship! Think! Who would do that??? Yes, the Devil! God is the good parent that says, "You have been wounded and hurt. You are in need of a Healer."

However, God will not make you rest from a broken heart; He will only advise you to do so. But if you will allow Him to take the time to heal you, the addictive desire for a "quick fix" will begin to leave you. You will never know what it is like to be well until you submit to God's care. Once you become well, your heart will never want to be sick again; therefore, you will not want to expose yourself to sick men. I have never seen a sick contagious person made well by a healthy person unless the healthy person was a doctor or a nurse with a prescription, but I have seen people who thought they were immune to sickness end up being contaminated by a sick person.

My point is to stay away from sick men and allow Doctor Jesus to work on you until you are healed. How do you know when you are healed or if you are in the process of being healed? Your desire to be in a relationship will change, and you will want more of God's Word; you will also want to live for God, not for what He can give you such a mate, but because you love Him. This takes time, but it will happen if you take your "meds" every day, for example: the Word of God, prayer, and the exercising your faith. You also must believe that God knows what is best for you. If you feel as though God is killing you, He is! That is just your flesh dying!

Does this seem too hard? Well, try dating an unsaved man or, better yet, a man pretending to be saved. He will beat your heart up so badly you will be begging God to heal you. Trust me...you don't want to go there year after year, repeating the same hurts over and over again. After a while, you become bitter, old, tired and used up. If you feel that way already, the good news is that God can still heal you. You will just have to decide to get off the cycle of abuse.

The night I wrote this in my journal, God gave me such a revelation of what I had been doing to myself over the last three years. As God was speaking to me, I was writing as fast as I could. I felt like God was transforming me right there on paper, right before my eyes. My journal entries were beginning to transform me from a victim mentality to a warrior's way of thinking. I took a break in the middle of the journal entry because it was so long. I actually wrote seven pages that night. This is when I finally realized that God was going to use me as well as my journal for ministry. There were times when I didn't want to write down my personal feelings anymore, but God continued to impress upon me to keep on writing in my journal.

September 6, 2005

(Continued)... Another way to know that God has healed you is for you to imagine yourself in a doctor's office, and for some this really has happened. You are taking an HIV test; many of you may know how unnerving that can be. In most cases, you have to wait for a week for the test results. That week can seem like the longest week of your life. Your mind begins to recall the fact that you slept with someone and did not use protection, and even if you did, something still could have gone wrong. Now, it's time to bargain with God and beat yourself up for what you have done. The next thing you do is re-evaluate your life and all the mistakes that you have made and ask God for a second chance. You vow to God that it will be different this time. The sun comes out, the birds start chirping, and God blesses your results. You are fine! Now what do you do? Do you go out and sleep with the first guy you get into a relationship with? No, you now have a newly found respect for yourself. Now that you understand that you are clean, no one is going to come in and dirty up your sheets that God has washed clean. You would be a fool to let someone do that to you sexually as well as emotionally. Well, that is how it feels when God heals you! If you do not sense that need to protect your heart and your body from the enemy, you are probably not healed.

God was beginning to open my eyes to the things around me. I was starting to get my joy back, but the Devil wasn't going to quit because I had gotten a revelation from God. As you well know, when God begins to plants good seeds, the Devil likes to cultivate bad weeds. He doesn't mind our getting a revelation as long as he can keep the weeds growing along with the seeds.

If it seems like my life was dragging on for me, try living it. I'm sure there are others that can relate to the drama of "single-hood" and the trauma of divorce. One minute you are full of life, and the next minute you are checking your cell phone for the tenth time in five minutes to see if you have received a text or missed a call. The Devil's plan is to either bore you to death so that you become desperate enough to go back to your old ways – in spite of what you know to be true – or to bring about distractions to lure you off the road to your destiny. Do not be surprised if you are up on the mountain for a few days and down in the valley the next. God is training your mind to be able to deal with both highs and lows. It is truly a process when you feel out of control; just know that God is still in control.

September 7, 2005

Thank you, Lord, for all you've done for me! I had a good day today. Thank you for allowing me to meet Tracy. God, I thank you for using her to give me gas money for my car. When I did her hair, I wasn't expecting anything from her, and that is what made it so nice. I love the way you are filling my house with new friends and old ones, too. My house is filled with the love of loved ones. I feel as though I am living again. I'm scared, but I am still happy.

I talked to Anthony at work today. He puzzles me with his actions. I have to remember that he has not received love or forgiveness from God, and he cannot give what he does not have. It is so easy to let the Devil ease his way back into my heart. My flesh enjoys his company, and I enjoy the attention he gives me, but there is that constant voice in my ear saying, "Danger! Stay away!" Anthony doesn't come to my job everyday, so it is hard to tell him to stay away. This is a tough one because he is always respectful to me and doesn't try to put his hands on me. I am not tempted to sleep with him, but I still get jealous of other women in his life. Why do I feel this way? I don't love him. I

*just want him to leave me alone and don't come around here any
more! Then, I miss him, but I get used to his being gone. Then here
he comes again tempting me with that contagious smile.*

*I was thinking about Anthony on the way back from dinner and
the reason why he dates so many women. He says that they become
boring to him, and he moves on, but what I have realized is that
Anthony is the one that has become boring. He leaves the woman
before she finds out how boring he really is. He doesn't want her
to know he has nothing more to offer her. We women get tired of
lying up in the bed having sex with someone who isn't our husband
and doesn't plan on marrying us. When we make demands on the
relationship, they get worried that we will reject them. So they will
say, "She is boring me." No, what it is, is that they have nothing else
to offer us but sex because they are not capable of loving us. They run
before we find out, but we chase them down with our unconditional
love. This scares the men to death because they know they don't love
us and have put so many conditions on us as well as themselves that
neither we nor they can measure up to having a relationship. Then
they begin to make up excuses after they have gotten our goodies
such as "I just wanted to be friends with you," "I'm too busy for a
girlfriend," "I'm not good for you," "I'm not in the place where I can
love you like you need to be loved," and my personal favorite, "I don't
think I'm capable of loving anyone."*

*I usually say they are scared of rejection and of giving themselves,
so they reject us before we reject them. Godly men can admit they
need God and a good woman, but ungodly men go from woman to
woman.*

I have an explanation for this journal entry! I was on a roll
that night. Remember you are reading from my personal thoughts
and the night of September 6, 2005. This is what I was thinking.
I don't want the men to think I am "male bashing" because I

am not. The men I am speaking about are the ones who know that they have no intention of being in a committed relationship with a woman, but they take advantage of the opportunity to hurt her or use her for their own selfish reasons. If this statement doesn't apply to you, then there is no reason to take it personally. However, if you are a gentleman reading this book and you used to be a player, you fully understand the games I'm talking about.

I have to beat up on us sisters, too, because we don't have to accept what is being served to us. I understand when we are hungry, we tend to eat from whatever plate that is being set before us. That is why it is so important that people, in general, should not allow their spiritual tanks to become low because they tend to go for the "fast foods" that, we know, have no nutritional value. The point I am making is that unequally yoked friendships, likewise, have no spiritual value.

I know that it is difficult to go without friends, especially male friends. However, the Devil loves to play games with us. He leads us to believe that we need to be friends with everyone or that we just need some companionship, not really a date. I have to admit that I was the poster child for men with whom I claimed, "I just wanted to be friends." I must say that the men in my life loved the idea. Gee, I wonder why?

I spent a lot of time looking at my cell phone, wondering why my friend had not bothered to call me. Didn't he miss me? I wasn't deceiving anyone but myself, and the only fool was me. I had once heard a preacher say that as Christians, "We are either coming out of a storm or in the midst of a storm or about to go into a storm at all times in our walk with Christ." Well, I was like these Christians. I was always coming out of a relationship or in a relationship or looking to be in a relationship. There was always this sense of not being content with God or with where I was with my life. I had fought that feeling for many years. I did not think that I could ever quench that fire for companionship. I can now tell you that it can be done! What is my secret? The Word of God!

Now let me explain: The world is full of suggestions such as T.V. commercials that suggest to you what you truly should desire. It could be as simple as a chocolate cake commercial that makes you feel like you just have to have it, even when you are clearly trying to lose weight. Well, the Word of God does the same thing for you. Because of the amount of technology today, there is no excuse for not listening to an encouraging word from the Lord. Every day when I wake up, I make a conscious choice of what to feed first, my spirit man or my flesh. I know my flesh will lie dormant if I do not feed it, and so I don't. I also know that my spirit man will grow stronger if I feed it, so I choose to feed my mind the Word of God. I listen to the Holy Spirit when it says that music is going to make me feel lonely or when a romantic movie is going to make me feel as if life has cheated me as well as others out of the love I deserve to have.

The Word of God is my bread of life. It tells me that I am loved by Jesus with an everlasting love: It tells me that God rewards those who diligently seek Him. The Word is my compass: It keeps me on track, especially when I am about to detour. I Corinthians 10:13 says, *"There hath no temptation taken you but such as is common to man: but God is faithful, who will not suffer you to be tempted above that ye are able, but with the temptation will provide a way of escape also so that you will be able to endure it."*

Now, I understand this is old school mentality, but, believe me, it works! The bottom line is that we have to eventually grow up spiritually in certain areas of our life because if we don't, God cannot take us into what He has planned for our future. We will not be able to hold onto that with which God is trying to bless us. Our character has to be able to sustain our blessing, or we will lose it every time. After some time has passed and disobedience continues, we will begin to feel as though God is ignoring our prayers to be blessed. He is not, but He will not change His protocol for us, no matter how long it takes us to conform to His plan for our lives. Remember, "He is the Father of time, but our time here on earth is limited."

Personally, I don't believe anyone who truly loves the Lord wants to spend his or her life repeating the same mistakes that were made when that person was in his or her early twenties, now that that person is thirty-five pushing forty years old. Enough mistakes will be made just living everyday life, but the choices are ours to make daily. We should choose the Word of God over regular T.V., whenever possible. We should turn off the secular music; it only fuels the desires of our flesh. We should make a choice to worship God both in our car and in our home. Yes, that is my secret; I put God first in everything I do. No, I am not perfect, and except for Jesus Christ, that person does not exist! But from many years of doing things the wrong way, I know that giving God 50% obedience and expecting to walk into 100% blessing from God doesn't work!

September 8, 2005

Lord, I thank you for allowing me to work another Saturday. I thank God for my job since I don't have any other social life. Well, I have a life with my girls and their friends, but not a life of my own. We had fun today. I took the girls to Bub's today, and they met up with their friends. From what I can tell, they are nice girls. From there, I went home, watched a movie with Ash, and then went to work.

I am amazed at the stories I have heard tonight. First, Tim and his situations and the fact that God kept him, and Mark and his problems, but he stood up for himself...yeah! And Sue and hers...I'm praying for all of them. Then I compare it to my life, which is simple, calm, and complete. I have sweet girls and a clean home; I live in a fabulous apartment and have good friends that would come over if I called. God has given me life and life more abundantly. Why is it so hard to be satisfied? With relationships come difficulties along with worry and fear like fear of "getting the short end of the stick."

The going to bed part when you get married seems to be the good part until you have to sleep with the person every night and he farts on you and doesn't shave, and his breath stinks, and then he wants to have sex with you without any romance. Men always seem so cool; they look and smell good when they are dating, but what is the deal when they have upset you all day and hurt your feelings and then that night want to make love to you?

When you are single with a good job, you don't have to share your money. You don't have to cook, if you don't want to. My kids are very understanding, and we are a family. I love not having to share them. I know that's selfish, but when you're single, you can be selfish. I still do get lonely, but God said He would supply all my needs, not wants, and He has. Compared to all my co-worker, I have the best life, and I am the most blessed! God, I thank you for taking the drama out of my life. You have finally given me peace! There is a reason why I am here in this place in my life. I may not fully understand why, but in due time, I will see the big picture! God, you never cease to amaze me! I love the way you work things out for my good.

This is a very unique entry. I was struggling with the idea of actually being happy. I know I should have been happy, but there was this nagging part of my heart that still wasn't satisfied. I knew how it felt to be married and all the difficulties that came with marriage, and I knew the freedom of being single with its share of problems like being loneliness or not belonging to someone on this earth, so I would talk to myself about how great it was to be single. I really didn't feel that way then, but it was almost like God was preparing me for what and how I would feel some day. I wanted to believe that I could have peace and be satisfied with what God was doing, but – to be totally honest – in my heart, I didn't.

Everything that I wrote in that last paragraph simply amazes me now as I transcribe the words into this book. I can honestly say He did replay every word of that entry and made it a reality in my life. All that I went through was for a purpose – this purpose – and He did work all things out for my good. At this time in my life, I can see the big picture, and God is the artist that has designed the picture. I believe God allowed me to go through the motions so that when others have to struggle down this same road, they will understand that where they are, is a part of the plan and process that God has for their lives.

September 11, 2005

God, I thank you for a beautiful day. I know this is a hard day for so many people. While we were celebrating at Indiana Beach, there were people mourning the loss of their love ones. I pray that they will receive their healing from you, precious Father, even those in New Orleans. You have been so good to the U.S. God, I know you love us...even love us enough to warn us on a small scale as well as a larger scale from coast to coast. Your message has always been so simple, "Love me, not other Gods; don't love man more than you love me." It takes us forever to get it, and still some never do.

I fought with the idea of whether to put this entry in the book, especially the part about God warning us, but as you may recall in the beginning of the book, I talked about the storms of life and how they are warnings for us to set our house in order. I believe God works in the natural as well as the spiritual. This is no disrespect to those who lost loved ones because I know how it feels to lose a loved one. I will go into detail about that later, but after a natural or an emotional storm blows into your life, you are never the same. The fact that my neighbor's house blows down and mine doesn't, does not give me the go ahead to continue business as usual…as if it were impossible for me to be a victim of the same kind of storm that damaged my neighbor's property. As a nation, when the South lost lives as well as the East, that was a warning to the North and the West to recognize God's awesome power and His mercy toward us as a nation.

September 21, 2005

In everything, give thanks. Tonight I got a ticket for going 61 in a 45-mile zone. God, I thank you for all the times you allowed me not to get tickets. I talked to Mary tonight, and she sounds just like me. I hear her say she is ready for change (love), but I hear God say not yet; that goes for me as well. I need to get the cruise ship out of my eye before I get the tugboat out of my neighbor's. It is a scary thing to know we're not quite ready for a relationship, but it's a good thing to know that God cares enough about us not to send us out there in the shape we are in. Some may say, "Why are there so many bad relationships in the church?" I would say we did that to ourselves because somewhere in the beginning stages of it all, God said no, and we stepped right over His still, small voice and gave ourselves permission to go full-steam ahead. As the years passed by, we forgot that we had disobeyed God; then the Devil came to collect… with interest.

Sometimes, it's eight or nine years later, and we think all is long gone and forgotten. That is why it is important to be mindful of our obedience to God. The Lord allowed me to know that He will put me with someone who has been through His process as well as through the fire. It wouldn't be fair to the other person if he got me and I was still "jacked up" on the inside and God had not changed the rude things about me. It wouldn't be right for someone to have to accept those things no more than it would be for me. I know there is a man out there praying for that good wife, too. I also know there are men and women who are praying for selfish expectations, and because they don't want to wait on God to heal them, they will end up finding each other, and that alone is a recipe for divorce.

The more God heals you, the better mate He has for you. I believe you are a reflection of your mate. It goes back to the list of qualities that you may want in a mate; you have to be sure that you can live up to the standards you hold others to.

I thank God for His Word and for allowing me to understand where He is taking me so that I can cooperate without doing it grudgingly. The first few times around, I obeyed because I felt like a kid on punishment; in order to get out of trouble with God, I would obey long enough for me to get out of the jail cell I thought He had me in. I don't think I really learned anything because all I could do was guess at what God was going to do. But as time passed, I stopped struggling and calmed down, and I began to receive the answers as to why I was here as well as what needed to change.

There is no faking it with God. If you want to get out of the prison, you have to come clean. With some people, it seems as if it takes a lifetime. I know a lot of people, including me, who say, "If I knew then what I know now, I know that I would have done things different."

I don't want to spend a lifetime trying to figure out what God has been telling me all along. The more we know the better witness we can be to the body of Christ.

There is suffering, but when we suffer with understanding behind it, it brings about purpose in our life. However, when we suffer due to lack of knowing better or disobedience, there is no purpose, and, most likely, we will repeat the same mistakes over until we come into the knowledge and obedience of Christ. Having that knowledge sheds light on our suffering and causes us to stop the disobedient behavior. We begin to grow spiritually, and we are then ready for the next challenge.

Sometimes, we are fully aware that we are doing wrong, but we feel as though we don't have any control over our actions. We want to stop, but we don't know how? It is because we have not fully given our will over to God. We are still trying to be in control and still serve God, too. It is a level of fear: fear of what will happen if we let go and let God have His way; fear of God's making us suffer for Christ. But what we don't understand is that we suffer for Satan when we don't summit to Christ; we will then spend the majority of our young adult life asking God why? God can sometimes become silent because we have not submitted to Him. It is easy to become frustrated with the silence and then sin more. Round and round we go! Then ten years go by (that would be all of our twenties), and we finally wake up and get a clue that God isn't going to change for us and that we must come into total obedience in order to have life and life more abundantly.

God was changing my thoughts. He was pouring fresh oil on my old wounds. This was the shifting point that allowed me to know that this was more than just a journal. I would write what God told me to write and then go back and read what I had written. I began to question myself and to ask, "Who wrote this?" I cannot take the credit for what God said to me. Some nights, the entries in my journal would be so long that my hand would hurt from writing, but I just could not stop. The knowledge was there, but I could not see the potential of what God was going to do in my life. I could only see my past. I knew the Word of God; I would study for two to three hours every night on my job; however, it wasn't going to make any difference in my life until I learned to completely trust and obey God in every area of my life.

What I didn't understand was that God was relentless in His pursuit for us. I thought I could select from a menu the things that I wanted to eat from the Word of God. I didn't know God was going to hold me accountable in every area of my life, even though this message had been repeated over and over by my pastor.

Jesus has the cure to our broken heart, and His Word is the balm that heals it. Oftentimes, we want to take the ointment out of God's hands and apply it to ourselves, because we feel as though our heart is too tender and sore for anyone else to touch it. The truth is that we are afraid to trust Jesus with our heart.

We have to give the balm back to Jesus and tell Him, "Lord, I trust you to apply this medicine to my heart. I have tried to put the medicine on myself, but my hands are infected with my own ideas and plans, but, Lord, I know you know what you are doing. You are still the great physician. Where else can I go? Who else can I trust?"

I have wasted so much time not completely trusting God. Now, if I don't understand why something is happening to me, either today or yesterday during my time with God, I still must trust Him. I trust that He loves me and that He knows what is going on with me. I trust that I am still the apple of His eye, even if I can't feel His presence. It is not about my feelings, because I have hormones! It is about what I know to be true about Him because, depending on what day of the month it is, I am from time to time all over the map. I know that God, undoubtedly, loves me 100%. He is not moody, and He is very merciful. I know that I am going to make mistakes; however, it is my responsibility to acknowledge them. I will go to Him and say, "I know what I did was wrong; furthermore, I am sorry! Lord, I receive your forgiveness." A wise woman named Joyce taught me that.

Chapter Eight

October 3, 2005

Good morning, Father. I haven't written in several days due to my bad attitude. I feel discouraged. It is harvest season, and I am ready for change, a good change! I don't like to write when I feel this way; however, I realize that it is important that I share both sides of my life because I do have low days as well.

I was listening to Max Lucuto's testimony about his five year journey into nowhere. One day he was up, and the next day he was down. What a story! My little sorrows are nothing in comparison. I always want to write something profound. I do have a lot of knowledge that you, Lord, have given me; however, it is useless if I cannot live it and digest it myself, and so the bad days have to come as well.

I was really down this past weekend. I had a nervous breakdown on Wednesday. Stephanie came by and gave me a card with a $140 in it! God is so good. She is a wonderful sister! I hugged her, cried, and thanked her. That doesn't sound like a bad weekend at all. I think it was just PMS. I felt overwhelmed and out of patience. Matter of fact, no matter what anyone else did or said, it still wasn't good enough. My heart was saying, "I want something big from God, a light at the end of my long cruel summer tunnel." But, I felt that if I *said that, I would sound selfish and ungrateful as well as unfaithful to God. And so a lot of my thoughts and emotions were building up to the point where I though I might explode, and that is exactly what I did! I cried Friday and Saturday. I let God have it! I believe if we are respectful, He listens. We need to complain aloud to God so that we can hear ourselves. It doesn't sound selfish in our minds; however, when it is spoken aloud before God Almighty, the Ruler of the Universe, it sounds completely different.*

It can begin with a good argument. We can be so sure that we are right, but because there is no one there to cut us off or discount our claim, we are able to get it all out. Then God begins to speak in that still, small voice in our mind. He says, "What, You don't trust me? You don't trust that I know what is best for your life?"

I reply, "I do, Lord, but I am human. I can only take so much."

And I can hear Him saying, "This is the fire!"

And I reply, "I hate the fire, but I know it is necessary because you wouldn't take me this way if it weren't." I resolve once again, "God, I know you know what is best, and you are always right." In the end, I'm mad. "I know I can't win, and even if you let me have it my way, I would lose."

I was not trying to go deep tonight, but somehow I always do. There is always wisdom in truth. Well, anyway it always helps when I write.

Sometimes, I just want to stay mad, but God won't let me; He humors me with His love and kindness. For example, on Sunday, Tommy Tenney was going to be at the night service at my church. I had worked the night before, and I came home in the morning, slept for a few hours, and then went to morning service. I came home and went back to bed. That evening, I overslept, and so I asked the Lord, "why didn't you wake me up?" I started not to go because it was 6 o'clock and the service had already started. I was thinking, "God you woke me up this morning...." Well, when I got to church Tommy Tenney was just getting up to preach. The usher lead me up to the front row next to my friend Neasha. Once again, I had to tell the Lord, "I'm sorry I was so crabby." So, yes, we still have those days when we are all over the map.

I tend to think that God uses those days for our good as well as to break down the walls that we build up in our wilderness experiences. The harsh, sandy winds cause us to want to put up walls to shelter us without really knowing what we've done. That is what I did...all summer long. I never really noticed it until I started crying and the walls began tumbling down with my tears.

I met a man on Sunday; I was so defensive he didn't stand a chance with me. I didn't want to play the game with him, but he was still nice to me in spite of my attitude. I was just plain mean to him. I knew once a person got to know the real me, I was not a mean person, but I felt like I needed to screen people even before they could become my friend.

I still have a lot of anger from what Craig and Prophetess did to me. I had not dealt with it in the early stages. I tried to just "let it go," as they say. I was letting it go with her (Prophetess) because I was trying to focus on healing from Craig. I was still missing him in the process. I found out he was not all that he had claimed to be and neither was she; after the way they talked about me, it was all I could take. So I began to stack my bricks...one by one...Anger and Betrayal. I didn't want to let people, like her and Craig in so that I wouldn't get hurt again. I really felt stupid; the two people who I really thought cared about me...

I can't heal myself, and so I lay my hurting heart at your feet, Jesus...piece by piece (it's broken, you know), or should I say shattered into a million pieces! It is painful, and I am angry, but by faith, I know I will be healed because God has worked on it before.

This was a hard entry to look back over. I once again give God the glory for my life. We sometimes relive many of the same hurts over and over. God performs many of the same healing procedures countless times in our lives. For some reason, whenever we are hurt in the same way by someone different, it is always a surprise to us. It is as if we don't think we will ever have to go through that particular trial ever again. Our options are limited. Either we can put up walls and never trust anyone, or we can trust God to heal us if we happen to be hurt once again by someone we have trusted.

I tried to do both, but it does not work that way. I am not saying that we should completely be an open book. The Bible tells us, *"Guard your heart with all diligence, because out of it comes the problems of life."* (Proverbs 4:23) However, God always has a purpose for our pain especially if He allows us to be betrayed by someone whom we would normally trust.

Oftentimes, God sends warning signs that allow us to know that there is danger coming in a particular relationship, and that is where Proverbs 4:23 comes in. If we ignore God's voice, then we suffer the consequences of our actions. Nevertheless, God is always faithful and loving. He offers us healing, if we are willing lay down our broken hearts at His feet.

The emotions that we are feeling on any given day are always temporary. Satan's plot from Hell is to discourage us. His job is to make us believe that God in addition to the so-called people that we considered our trustworthy friends has abandoned us. However, God is not like man, nor is He to be compared with man. He can be fully trusted…even if we think He is hurting us. God is always working the pain out in our lives for our good.

The present times in which we live are very difficult times. God is preparing us to be able to withstand the fire of tainted relationships, as well as perplexed emotions that are the result of them. The more we are exposed to the fire of God, the stronger we become as Christians. God has to lay a foundation eventually in our lives, and it usually begins with that first major betrayal. We often do not recognize God's hand in the fire because we are too busy trying to expose the perpetrator to anyone who will listen to our sorrows and pain. That is why journals are so helpful; they allow us to vent and to talk to God all at the same time. Journals allow us to reflect on our journey and on God's goodness. Journals also bring about consistency between our mistakes and God's grace in caring for us, even when we disobey Him and fail to trust Him. When we reflect, it becomes very clear to us how much God truly loves us and how patient He is with us even when we are not patient with Him.

October 5, 2005

"I'm so secure. You're here with me. You stay the same. Your love remains here in my heart… so close. I believe you're holding me now in your arms. I believe you'll never let me go."

That is how I feel today, renewed by your grace, love, and healing power. Every time I hear your Word, you tell me something I haven't heard before as well as the same things I've heard over and over. "I love you, Lori. I have a future for you. Trust me, Lori." I reply, "I do." Sometimes, my actions betray me, and then I hear your Word, the one thing that brings me back to reality. There are times when encouragement makes me mad, for instance, when Charles Stanley talks about God supplying all our needs in his southern drawl. I just want to scream because I know it's true, although it doesn't feel true right now...at three in the morning. I am lonely, crying, and feeling very confused.

He just wasn't doing it for me. He actually made me even madder. So I went back to the library to get more tapes. I'm not sure what I am looking for, but no more "it's-going-to-be fine tapes."

I stumbled across a tape called "The Spirituality of Waiting." It talked about how we were always waiting on a response from someone and how we could not make a person respond the way we wanted him to respond. We would just have to wait and see how he or she would respond. The tape spoke of a man who was used to responding to others his whole life. It made him feel in control. He was then stricken with cancer, and he became the person who was waiting for someone to respond to him. His point was when we worship what we do more than who God is we lose our focus. However, when God makes us wait for Him, we have to wait for His response to us. We cease to be in control anymore. It is an undesirable place to be, and we want to run away or leave, but if we have been with Jesus or around the mountain several times, we will learn to wait, no matter how much it "sucks." Well, it had taken me three years to get a hold of this truth.

He went on to say, "To wait is a form of passion." This was before <u>The Passion of the Christ</u> came out in theatres. When we wait on God, we are entering into a passion or a love for Him. If He could wait 38 years on me, then why can't I wait six months on Him?

Many times Jesus uses the simplest stories to teach us profound messages. He uses parables all throughout the four Gospels. Through God's Word, He does the same for us. We should not discount a small nugget of wisdom from our pastor or even from a wise, older saint. We need to take time to really hear and discover the wisdom that lies just beneath the surface.

October 11, 2005

*Lord, I give you the praise! Thank you for allowing me to write the first chapter of my book. I could hear you guiding and directing my words in each sentence. It's funny! Lord, I don't know how this book is going to end. I do know it is **an expected end**. Sunday I got called out in the service. I was hoping I would. It is usually a good thing at Overcoming. The Lord told me he was going to call me up there, and thirty seconds later Pastor Farr did. He told me that the Lord was going to restore to me everything that I had lost. Let's see, I had lost my home, my car, my husband, my stability, my heart, my business, and my faith. He also said, "Don't think that you missed His voice and stop feeling condemned all the time. Allow God to take you to another level."*

Chapter Nine

Lord, I thank you for a beautiful day. I thank you for looking out for me. I bow down to your awesome power; you are the King of my life, my heart, and my world. I am not sure if I am ready to let anyone into our world...our space. I don't want to share you. Well, I do, but...you know what I mean!

Last night, Neasha, Stacy, and I were talking about men. We were talking about what we liked and disliked. I don't even remember how Jordan's name came up, but I asked Neasha if he ever feels like a woman feels? Does he ever get lonely or tired of being alone because most men I know love the lifestyle of being a bachelor?

Well, Neasha said he does get lonely and he does want to get married.

I said, "He does? Neasha! Jordan is your husband!" and we all had a good laugh.

Neasha said, "No, he's your husband."

I replied, "No he's too young for me, plus he dated one of my best friends and my sister. That is double no, no!"

The next day Dad called me to tell me Jordan wanted to talk to him about me. What! Ever since I had that conversation with Dad, I have been off the chain! I have reasoned in my mind about this man. He is too young…and too big! I can't have someone younger than me who has never experienced marriage telling me what to do! I don't need a daddy…or a son! I need someone to live my life with. I don't know when I will change my mind about someone telling me what to do. I will soon be forty years old. I don't want any one telling me how to spend my money or what kind of car I should drive.

O.K., I was in one of those moods. I think it was PMS! I typed this entry, and then I hit the backspace because I thought it was pointless until I read the next entry. Every time I try to omit something stupid that I have said, the Lord tells me to put it back in the book. At this point, I believe I was still suffering from my break up with Craig. He had been somewhat opinionated, and had suggested to me I needed a bigger car for him and his sons. Read on…!

October 20, 2005

Lord, I thank you for my life and for my freedom in you. This week has been a test to see if I have matured in you. I feel as though I passed the test. (To God be the glory!) Tim was laid off for ten days, so I had to run his job. Everyone, including me, thought I would fall apart, but I never let them see me sweat. I got some exercise, and I learned the job. I'm sore but I don't mind. It's even my PMS week! You know, God is good!

I re-read my last entry about Jordan. I have been driving myself loony about this situation, and I haven't even talked to him yet! He hasn't even asked me out, but I am jumping to all of these conclusions about him mostly based on hearsay. I don't think he is for me, but maybe I'm judging wrong. I don't want to start anything that has the potential of going bad. I keep wondering, "God, do you have someone special for me? Am I supposed to bypass this for what you have, or is this what you have? Are you going to take black and white paint and make it yellow? Lord, I sound as crazy as I did back in 2002! But, Lord, I can't afford to make anymore bad choices. I know you will let me know. I don't want to be closed minded, but I also have certain expectations, and he doesn't seem to fit into those expectations."

I cannot believe I don't mind being alone. I guess I have days when I am bored, but for the most part, it's not that bad. I'm glad winter is coming. I am expecting great things this winter. I will be working on my book all snuggly in the house next to the fireplace. I never thought I would be glad for that. Oh, yeah, and I'm not desperate anymore (random thought), and this concludes my rambling session for this week.

One of the things I love about God is the fact that He can use us even when we are not completely healed. Otherwise, there would be no one for God to use. I was in the midst of being healed, but my old nature was still alive. I am a thinker, and I tend to analyze everything to death. This thing about Jordan was driving me nuts because, in my mind, I was still obsessed with finding a mate, even though I kept telling myself I didn't want anyone. One minute I did. The next minute I didn't.

What I really wanted was peace in my mind. I also had not learned to completely rest in God. I believe we all struggle in that area of our life. If it isn't a mate, it's a job, a car, a house; it is so hard to be satisfied. I believe that part of our struggle has to be walked out by faith, but I also know God can heal us in the mist our walk. As for me, it took seven years. I pray that all those who read this book understand that we all have struggles in our lives. These struggles will be worked out in God's time not ours. God will not change his plan for our lives to relieve us from the pain of our struggles; however, he will use them to strengthen our character so that we can help others to overcome their problems.

I did not want to put this entry in the book, but I did it out of obedience to my heavenly Father. Read on…!

October 25, 2005

To God be the glory for the things He has done in my life! This was the week that I usually lose my mind, crying over the latest breakup while asking God, "Why? God why did he have to break up with me? What's wrong with me?" Though I must admit the Devil did come with his mess as he did last month and I could feel the pangs of loneliness starting to kick in my door of belief, I really do believe God. And my love for Him has become much greater than any pain He allows me to feel.

I began to offer up my past hurts to Him as a living sacrifice. I understand this level of pain because I have felt it before, and it isn't going to kill anything but my flesh. This pain fuels me to abide in my Comforter Jesus even more and to worship harder. I want a clean heart and clean sheets. There is no pain a man has given me that could ever cause me to want to go back to where I was before. God has brought me out of it for my good, and so I thank Him for knowing what is best for me. This is called trusting God.

Sometimes, I can't think too long about trusting God before Satan comes along with his reasons and maybes and doubts, and so I just do what God says. I thank Him before I have a chance to replace my thoughts with the thoughts of the enemy. If I let him ride, he will want to drive me crazy with thoughts of doubt. He will make me think I can't hear from God and make me think maybe I didn't hear this or that from God. i.e. The Lord told me to use another gate when I entered work, and so I obeyed God, but when I would be running late, it was quicker to go in a different gate (the one He had told me not to use). When I did, I would run into Anthony and talk to him, and immediately after, I would feel conviction. This happened several times. I was now sure of what God had said about that gate. He was trying to heal me of my past hurts. Ex-boyfriends don't usually bother me, but when I see Anthony, my flesh wants to resurrect itself, and it seems as if I have to start all over again. I can't totally heal if I keep exposing myself to my old flame… as well as new ones. They all still burn. So when God tells us to do something, even though it doesn't seem significant, it is better to just obey Him. God doesn't care how sanctified we think we are. He would rather that we obey Him.

Jordan didn't e-mail me. I wasn't surprised. I felt like God was saying he was not the one. I probably scared him away. Who knows? I will talk to him and find out when I see him. I recommend that he read the book I Kissed Dating Goodbye . This book really expressed what I was trying to say to Jordan, but he didn't get it. I believe he will in due time. I know he's a good guy, but he's not as ready as he thinks he is, plus he wants kids, and I can't do that for him. The whole thing makes me somewhat sad because he is saved, and it is hard for me to wait on God. I feel like a criminal that just got out of prison. I want to do right, but it is so hard.

You know, we often wonder why criminals who have been in prison for 20 years get released from jail and go back to their old lifestyle. Common sense says don't go back to the streets because that is how they got in trouble in the first place. But if they don't know anything but the streets, it's hard not to keep committing the same crime. They don't want to go back to jail, so then what? They have to learn new skills. They have to learn how to function in the outside world and make a living without committing a crime to pay for it.

Well, in my past, God would put me on lockdown, meaning He wanted me to focus on Him only, no dating or phone calls from men, sort of like a sabbatical, which would usually last around four months. I would always be obedient during that time. I would become really close to God. My phone wouldn't ring, and no men would ask me out. Then all of a sudden, the prison door would once again open, and I would meet someone and think, "He has to be the one that God has for me. Why would God allow for me to meet him after all of these months of solitude?" I would leap before asking God because I was so happy to be out of my prison cell of loneliness and solitary confinement, only to go back to the streets of regular life to commit the same crime that would send me back to my prison of loneliness that I hated so much. So this time, it has been 5 ½ months, and in two weeks it will be six months. The last boyfriend I had cost me 6 months in the slammer.

The prison guard has come to tell me I am out on parole. And, of course, there is (big and sort of sexy) Jordan to pick me up at the prison gate. But I can hear God saying, "He is not the one," but I say to God, "I'm out of prison, and all I know is what has always been familiar to me. I've got men coming out of the woodwork after me, and I am like a crack head in a crack house, or a kid in a candy store."

God says, "Just because it's there doesn't mean you have to go after it." All of this is new to me, this trying to be obedient to God's voice. When I was in solitary confinement, I could hear God's voice so clearly, because it was just God and me. Confinement was a quiet place. I wanted to fight it at first, but then I became one with God. I soon realized that He was the only one with a key, and if there was any chance of my getting out, it was through Him.

I began to pray, "Please, God, let me out!" He was silent, so I cried even louder, and yet He remained silent. Then I fasted, and

He was still silent, but somehow in my weakness, God had begun to make me strong. My flesh was dying to His will, now that I had used up all of my old resources, meaning the things that used to work in the past. I realized that God was doing a new thing. Now that I had finally surrendered (that is the part I forgot about), God spoke in a still, small voice. Maybe I would have heard earlier if it weren't for all that crying and begging I was doing. But now I was like a child who was all cried out, and now I was ready to listen and obey.

Well, my time was up, and I was out of my prison. What was going to be different about this time? I had been to jail so many times for the same crime; what had I learned this time that I hadn't learned last time I was in jail? There was always a new revelation every time I went in there, but when I got out and was faced with the same choices, what would I do? Well, I could steal away with God every day and not stop doing what I was doing when He had me on lockdown; the world out there was a bigger prison than the cell where God had had me. There is safety inside the walls of God, and the cell I once thought was a prison was really a "city of refuge." Once we leave the refuge of God's walls, it takes a lot more effort to get back into His city. Fortunately, I now have a key to get back in, the key is called obedience.

I must listen to everything He tells me and walk according to the steps He has ordered for me. The first time I decide to disobey creates a "Y" in the road. If I decide to disobey God, then the "city of refuge" begins to change back into prison walls right before my eyes. But if I decide to repent and listen to God every day and allow Him to make every decision, it becomes my freedom. God loves it when we walk close to Him. He loves our neediness. If I feel myself going back into my old ways, it means that I am not listening to His voice or that I am just reasoning it away. It is better to just obey; obedience is the key to God's city of peace.

Chapter Ten

November 6, 2005

Lord, I bless your holy name! Thank you for a fantastic weekend in Chicago! I sat in the room with millionaires and people who made thousands of dollars through a company called Pre-Paid Legal Legal Legal. I had the best time, and I feel so alive! I have been in seclusion for so long that this venture was like a breath of fresh air. When God said, ***"I know the plans I have for you,"*** *He wasn't kidding. Yes, I am struggling financially, but God has given me a vehicle by which I can ride my way out. God, I thank you for not forgetting me. I have been waiting on my change for 3 ½ years. I don't know where I am going just like Abraham didn't, but, God, I know you know! Between my close walk with God, my book, and Pre-Paid Legal Legal, there is no room for anything else.*

Tomas called me, and I was glad to hear from him, but I am happy with the way things are in my life…less distractions. God is truly doing a work in that area of my life; every time a controlling guy tries to get close to me, I'm ready to escape the other way. I don't want to be tied down to a dictator. Not all men are like that, but I seem to draw out the Hitler in them. I'm attracted to the quiet type, but the loud controlling men always seem to seek me out, and then they get mad when they can't control me. God, I just thank you for my life with the girls. I want to see them succeed in life. God, please help me to be a positive force in their lives; please show me how to help them with their grades.

This was a very exciting time in my life. I had been on a six-month sabbatical, trying to heal from my breakup with Craig. I think this was the longest break I had taken from life…at least the social part of it. I believe a lot of people have those times in their lives when they drop out of sight from everyone. It is a time of reflection, prayer, and healing, but they must remember Satan is waiting for them. He doesn't mind how long they spend with God, as long as he can have some of their time, too. The Devil knows patience is a virtue, and that is probably the only virtue he is interested in. So there he sits at the gate of the prison, waiting for us to walk out with our new lease on life.

I was so excited about the new business in which I was getting involved. Desperate for a social life, I was also trying to be very careful of the company I was keeping. It is very hard to balance our personal time with God with our time in the business of the world, but it is necessary that we do; otherwise, we will find ourselves once again drifting out to the sea.

November 22, 2005

There is no way I can live without you. Thank you, Jesus, for a good life. I thank you for enlarging my territory. This is the winter season, but it feels like summer. All the seeds that I planted this past summer have started to grow. I can see little green sprouts growing all over my beautiful garden. I see some weeds popping up, too, but if I tend to my garden every day, I can pull up those weeds before they take over my fruit. I water my garden with the living water of prayer and worship, and I feed and nourish my garden with the Word of God. The more I tend to my garden, the easier it is to manage.

Lord, I thank you for the new life you have given me. Lord, I have been so busy, but not too busy for you. You are my source; I would be a fool to cut off the one who is supplying all my needs. I was talking to Francine earlier, and we were talking about being insecure in friendships, especially with men. I was telling her that is how I felt in the last relationship I was in. I told her how he tricked me into thinking that he was the one that was insecure so that I would let down my guard and stop guarding my heart with all diligence. Then, I began to feel sorry for him.

He told me that he couldn't afford to be hurt again. I was thinking to myself, "Good! He knows exactly how I feel; we have a good understanding of each other's pain in past relationships."

As time progressed, our relationship began to shift, and I was taking on the role of the one who had to prove that I was worthy of being with him because, of course, his feelings were more important than mine. I had to prove to him more and more that I loved him and that I wouldn't hurt him. The whole time I was doing this, I didn't realize that I was sinking into the trap of insecurity. With every false accusation that he made toward me, I became more insecure about myself. I always had to defend my character and myself. I was starting to think I wasn't good enough for him. I let go of God and totally trusted him, and I fell really hard.

And then he began to have this smug air about himself, as if he had played this game before...the game of manipulation. I began to wonder if I would ever heal from all this pain. For six months, I was in the Word, praying and trying to get past this horrible nightmare with this man that I loved with all my heart. I told God I would not date another man until He healed me from this pain. During that time in my life, Craig called me, not enough to want me back, but just enough to drive me insane and keep me insecure.

As the months went by, the love I felt for this man just would not subside. Believe me, I prayed for God to take it away. I couldn't understand why it wouldn't go away, especially after four or five months. Then God began to show me why.

During the time I was in pain, I was drawing closer and closer to God. The pain was what drove me into God's arms. God was becoming a strong force in my heart and in my life. I was leaning heavily on God for everything. God took Craig's place in my life. Craig should have never had that place to begin with. It always belonged to God. God just took back what rightfully belonged to Him in the first place. When I made that vow to God about not dating another man, I was really waiting on Craig. I didn't know that he was seeing other women in the church; that is the nicest way I can put it.

Now there is no one but Jesus and me, and for the first time in my life, I am free! I am secure because nobody can outweigh my relationship with God.

You know, when we were teenagers, we never really worried about a guy breaking up with us because there was always that one guy who always loved us no matter what. He was the one that we would call when the one we claimed to love, broke our heart. With Jesus, it is so much better. He is the first and the last. No man can even compare to the Lover of my Soul. A man can play games or walk away from me, but he will always lose because my relationship with God is the only relationship that I can't live without. How do I know this? I have been without a husband, and I am still here. I have been left at the altar, but I am better for it. But when I left God, I had nothing because He is my security. Without Him, there is no other security. We wonder why we feel so insecure when we put our trust in man; there is nothing to take his place if something goes wrong. *Jesus said, "I will never leave you or forsake you." We can always trust Him because in Him there is no insecurity.*

Wow! This entry came as a surprise to me. When I am transcribing the journals, I do not always read ahead. I read things as I type them on my computer. A lot of my entries, I haven't read in over four to seven years, so it is like reading them for the first time. I had completely forgotten about the part that I had written about Craig and how insecure he made me feel. I guess this journal entry is pretty self-explanatory.

November 27, 2005

*Happy 39ᵗʰ Birthday to me! Lord, I thank you for allowing me to live half of my life if I live to be 78 years old. I believe the best is yet to come. God, I love you! I shouldn't be alive; it is only by your grace that I am here. It's only because you have plans for me and **an expected end**.*

Lord, I thank you for another day of mercy. I have been going through all week long with my family. I ask you for forgiveness. I don't want my pride and selfishness and stupidity to take over my Garden of Eden. I have weeds popping up everywhere. I am going to pull them tomorrow morning. God, I ask that you prepare me for tomorrow. Give me a clean heart to do the right things to make amends with the loved ones in my family and to walk in integrity. I want to be blessed like Daniel, Joseph, and Esther.

November 30, 2005

To God be the glory for the things He has done! It has been an interesting week. I have gone from 0 to 60 and back so quickly. Lord, I thank you that I have you to lean on as my life becomes an emotional battle, now that I have to deal with the real world and all the people who live in it. Lord, there is so much drama it is crazy! I constantly have to refer back to your grace and mercy and the fact that you have me where I am supposed to be. When I was alone all summer, there was so much peace in my life. I lived like a hermit. Then, I came out of my shell into this busy "dog-eat-dog" world. Nothing can ever prepare us for dating, trying to stay pure, trying to live with a clean heart, treating mean people with kindness, and not falling for a male of any kind! The noise of this world tries to drown out your voice, and it's hard to hear you clearly. I hate making mistakes, God. I want to walk close to you and be obedient, but when I do, I become judgmental toward others because their walk isn't like mine. Lord, help me to understand that failure will come sometimes. I get so afraid that if I fall, the consequences will not allow me to get up fast enough. I feel as though I have reaped nothing but misery through my mistakes. Lord, I'm scared to make any more mistakes. I don't want to reap any more pain in my life. I feel like you have set me free, but when I am free, I have to go back into the real world where there is nothing but drama and mistakes waiting to happen. How do I occupy my time? I have mastered the DVR, watching T.D. Jakes and Paula White, and in my car listening to Joyce Meyer and Elder Farr's tapes as well as listening to worship CD's. But as soon as I begin to venture out as I am with Pre-Paid Legal, everything begins to move so fast. I want to learn everything there is to know, but I feel guilty because I am not getting as much Word as I was when I was sitting in my room every night.

Lord, I want you to know that I love you very much, and I need to ask myself am I putting anything in front of you. It is really easy when I am alone and all I have is God, but when opportunity is placed in front of me and there is nothing to keep me from it, keeping God first becomes a challenge. God, I thank you for the road blocks that require me to give you all the glory. I want that Joseph and Abraham success. They had success in all that they did, but for me and everyone else, it is going to be a bumpy ride to success, and I want to be the first one there.

Lord, I ask that you help me to find balance. Send people who need PPL services and help them to prosper, too... or even more. Bless Rick and Charlene to get it together. I don't like being in the middle of their drama. I find myself drawn to Rick because he is smart and has a great level of integrity, but then I feel guilty. Lord, help me and help me to help others.

December 14, 2005

Lord, I thank you for yet another good day! I remember a time when I couldn't say that. My life was a train wreck, but piece by piece, you have begun to put my life together again. It has been a slow painful process that I have prolonged due to my disobedience. I thank you for each day because it becomes my point of reference; where there is no struggle or pain, there is no glory, and God you deserve all the glory! The way that I take seems normal to me, but to others, I seem to be strange. Lord, I love you, and I pray that I stay in your will because it feels awful when I'm not.

December 19, 2005

Wow! I can't believe this year is almost over! This has been a defining year for me. Lord, I thank you. What the Devil meant for my evil, you have certainly turned into my good. I have practically spent the whole year grieving over Craig – praying for him, loving him, proving myself to him. It is so unbelievable! It just wasn't right, yet he caused me to grow spiritually by leaps and bounds! He caused me to leave my den of iniquity, yet we turned around and created our own. He was the one I thought I had been waiting for all my life, but what I found out was God was the one I had been looking for all along. Yes, a part of me still loves Craig very much, but I had to make a choice. We all do. For God I live, and for God I die!

Craig helped me through a simple statement he had made: "I need God more than I need a woman." I just took his statement and flipped it. I don't think I had really known that before. I might have said it solely to impress others, but I really don't think I believed it. But over the summer, God proved that it was true. After all that I had been through, I realized that God was my only source. I would have never thought I could walk this path without royally screwing it up.

God, I thank you for rescuing me from myself. God, I ask that you save Craig and heal him of all his issues. I thought I could be there for him. He told me that he was not good for me, but I would not listen. I wanted him to be well, but he isn't. I can't even be friends with him; it's hard to love someone that can't love you back. Besides…I am still terribly attracted to him. I can't be alone with him. Well, enough about Craig! Blah! Blah! Blah!

Chapter Eleven

HAPPY NEW YEAR 2006!

January 3, 2006

"And to all things there is a season." Lord, I thank you for carrying me through another year. Craig came over Christmas Day, doing the same junk he has done for the past 8 months or more. It's really been almost a year in February. Once again, he lied to me and tried to break my heart again. But the Mender of Broken Hearts protected me...even in my stupidity. I went to Atlanta to get away. When I was on my way home, I asked God, "Please don't let me return home the same way I left." God began to touch my heart on that ride home. I believe that trip to Georgia and Alabama was meant for me. It was the most peaceful trip I have ever been on. I know God was with me on the way there and on the way back.

The Devil never gives up when he thinks he has an opportunity. He knew my heart was still bruised from my relationship with Craig. The Devil is relentless in his pursuit for our souls, so we must be relentless in our pursuit for our freedom. He is constantly trying to wrap the chains of bondage around our lives. He is angry because God has set us free. Soon after I made the statement, "For God I live and for God I die" on December 19, he was at my door on Christmas morning. Who visits their ex-girlfriend at five o'clock in the morning on Christmas Day without first calling? Nobody but the enemy!

Life has many twists and turns and seems to repeat itself over and over again. As I write even now and read though my 2005 journey, I can't help but think that I revisited the same places in 2007 and 2008 that I did in 2005. It is amazing how our emotions will continue to rise and fall like mountains and valleys. I don't want to give anything away, so I will leave that alone for now.

The next entry you are about to read had been brewing since the day Rick recruited me for Pre-Paid Legal Legal Legal at the mall. Let me explain. Drama is always awaiting anyone who is willing to jump in bed with it. Rick and Charlene was a dysfunctional couple. They claimed to love the Lord, but they were no different from any other Christian couple who had not make God the "three-cord strand" in their relationship. They were constantly fighting, and she was extremely jealous of me. I could not understand why, but later down the road, I was going to find out why.

January 3, 2006 (contd...)

Rick and I had a serious talk. I told him what the Lord told me to say concerning his holding up his blessings from God. I prayed for him and Charlene. I really feel bad at times for her. She seems as though she feels left out, and she is as struggling to hold onto Rick. I sometimes think they don't belong together, but that could very well be my flesh. That remains to be seen. I just know, if we recognize God but then we choose our sinful lifestyle over obedience to God, it usually doesn't work out. That has been my personal experience. God always requires that we put Him first. I have to wonder if Charlene loves God or Rick or if she claims to love both. Rick says he loves God, but he doesn't want to hurt Charlene, so he compromises for her and takes himself out of the will of God.

I want our Pre-Paid Legal Legal Legal team to be successful as well as to be proud of Rick because he brought me into the business, but he won't have much unless he becomes obedient to God. We have the strangest friendship. There are times when I think it is going in the wrong direction, and then we both have to back off. We start to miss each other and start talking again. We never discuss anything but Pre-Paid Legal Legal... except for our last conversation concerning his spiritual life. Somehow, we end up talking for an hour or so and feeding off each other's ideas. I feel so guilty for talking to him, and so I back off. I certainly don't want to be the other woman.

Kelvin

Kelvin was a Pre-Paid Legal Legal legal employee. He was always antagonizing me, and I would do my best to ignore him. He would sit behind me at the meetings and say little annoying things, and it was my job to ignore his behavior. After three months of treating Kelvin as if he didn't exist, I decided to be cordial. One day, I was talking to one of the ladies after the meeting when he walked up and interrupted our conversation. We were talking about the Lord, and I was encouraging her not to give up. For some reason, Kelvin looked disheartened. When she walked away, he stayed and formally introduced himself. He asked me what church I attended, and I told him.

I asked him if he went to church. He said "yes," and he was a minister. He said he was raised at a church called Grace Apostolic.

I said, "I know a lot of people from Grace, but I don't ever remember your being there. Did you say a minister? I would have never guessed...a minister for real?"

He began to tell me his wounded puppy-paw story. I listened as he whimpered. As he was telling me his story, tears began to roll down his face; it was as if he were "the Prodigal Son." I thought at that moment; anyone who comes to me with a sincere heart deserves at least a chance to be heard. It was getting late, and the meeting was over, so we began to head toward the exit.

When we arrived at the door, we noticed the rain was falling heavily. Kelvin told me to wait at the door; he darted out in the rain and came back with the biggest umbrella I have ever seen. He proceeded to walk me to my Jeep. When we got there, I thanked him and said goodnight. Kelvin then asked me for my number, and I told him, "No, I usually don't give my number out, but I will take your number, and I will call you."

Left without an option, he agreed. I can't really say how long I made him wait for that call because I can't honestly remember. He was very nice to me when we started talking, but I was extremely guarded because of my past. It was hard to read him because we weren't actually dating...just friends, but then he would flirt with me and send me mixed signals. He would invite himself to my house for dinner at least three to four times a week. I told him he needed to buy groceries because I couldn't afford to feed another child. To this day, I didn't know how I got to this place...I was drifting like a ship without a sail.

February 15, 2006

Well, it's the day after "V" Day. I always meet someone right before this holiday...but not on purpose. It just happens that way.

I thank God for my life, and I always have to give Him the honor and the praise, and I thank Him for my family. I can't believe Brian is gone. It has been horrible for Francine, but I believe that she will make it through. My life has changed so much this year.

I met Kelvin; we have our ups and downs, but right now my stomach is in knots. I don't know if I am extra sensitive or if it's just him. He has on his game face. Sometimes I feel as though he's preoccupied (and he is) with his situation. He doesn't always give me what I need emotionally; he is with me, but he's really not. He is always complaining, yet he says that is what I do. Am I crazy or is he? He loves his laptop more than he loves Jesus; the only attention I get is when I am doing something for him like riding around in my car burning my gas for him, fixing his laptop, or surfing from page to page online for him. I am going to give him a limited time to see how things progress. I don't like the way I feel when I get off the phone with him. I realize that he is going through a lot of things, but I have already been through so much. I don't think I could bear going through what it would take for us to make it. Then he says those flattery words that reel me back in again, and the ugly process starts all over again. Men know what to say to get what they want.

Why is it so hard for me to trust? I feel as if I have caused half of my own heartache just from bringing up the past. Because of what others did to me in my past, it was hard for me to tell the difference, so I decided not to trust anyone.

All the signs that he was not the one were there, but because I had already been through so much, I assumed that I would not have to fight anymore. I was tired; furthermore, I felt as though I deserved to be blessed…after all that I had endured. I kept depending on the fact that he was a preacher and that preachers were more complicated. I rationalized everything and gave the

Devil more time than he deserved. I was in the boxing ring with the Devil once again, and there was no way I was going to win.

February 23, 2006

God, I thank you for your mercy endures forever. February has been an emotional month for me. Thank you, Lord, because your ways are not my ways. I thank you for your mercy and your patience. I don't do well with sin in my life. When my source is cut off, I suffocate. You are the air that I breathe. I look for Kelvin to be my air supply; he can't see that I am dying from the loss of air; I reach for him to help me breathe…Isn't that what preachers do?but he can't. He only has enough oxygen for himself. God is my source. I struggle with sin, and I walk in flesh, and flesh is death to me. I feel myself die a little every day. I want him to not lead us that way; I want him to be responsible for my soul and his. I want him to lean toward God; then I can lean with him, but he keeps losing me in the turn. I am afraid to lean his way because I do not want to lose my soul and my relationship with God. Therefore, I am always complaining and needing reassurance that he is on the right track.

I need to be responsible for my own soul, but then I feel selfish… as if I'm leaving him out there to die. Who is the strongest, he or I? I am having trouble deciphering my role. I am the one providing, yet he calls himself the head? I'm the giver, yet he is supposed to be my protection. My kids are mad at me, and yet I am angry with them. It seems like everyone wants something from me. I am all tapped out! I have spent hundreds of dollars on the kids and the household, etc., yet it is never enough. I never hear "Thanks, Lori!" or "Thanks, Mom!" It is always "Why can't you do more?" or "Mom, I'm hungry!"

I feel as if I could keel over dead and no one would care. Someone would just shake me to see if I am still alive so I can hand out yet another dollar, drive someone somewhere, or pick someone up. I always thought whenever someone came into my life, he would be there to help me and to take the pressure off me, not to add more or demand more! I have my kids for that! I find myself emotionally starved and disappointed most of the time: Then, I see him with his kids and his mom and others, and he is very nurturing. I deserve to be nurtured, too.

If I ask him to be there for me, he accuses me of complaining and acts as though I'm getting on his nerves. Doesn't he realize that I need attention? The reason why people enter into relationships is to share each other's burdens. I feel as if I am carrying the whole load. I know it's not all true because Kelvin has his own load. I guess I need him to carry some of mine. I am supposed to be the weaker vessel; I carry part of his, so why can't he carry some of mine? He makes me feel so selfish asking for help, love, or reassurance from him, and then he scolds me like a child and tells me that I should understand his shortcomings and his predicaments.

I still can't get any help. Where is my soldier…my man who has my back? That is why women are becoming strong where men are supposed to be. They are tired of leaning on men, only to fall. There are only so many times we are going to fall before we get up and start rebuilding that wall around us so that we can have something to lean on. I look forward to the day when T.D. Jakes preaches on this… yeah! We are loosed, but we still need the shoulders of our men!

Whew! That was a lot of fussing, but I had to get it all out! I was furious with this man! I was trying to make something work that clearly was not in God's will. When the Devil brings it, he brings it. Kelvin was a combination of both Derrick and Craig. I was getting two for the price of one! This just proves that I can't ride down the same road and expect to see different scenery. I thought I had changed, and I believe that I had, but my circumstances had not changed. I was still lonely, frustrated, and determined to get my break-through, no matter what it cost me. I was in a place of bewilderment and on the edge of despair. I could never understand why I had tried so hard for so long and still could not move God to bless me the way I wanted to be blessed. All I had ever wanted was stability, a husband to love, and someone to love me back. I could not see the big picture, and I had now run out of faith.

Chapter Twelve

June 13, 2006

Thank you, God, for all that you have done for me. I have not written in four months. Things with Kelvin ended up like all the other relationships. They all wanted me and wanted to be with you in the beginning, but when I decided I wanted them, too, suddenly, that was too much to ask for. I was acting insecure, and I was pressuring them. They were generally the ones who started out aggressively toward me, and then they gave me their expectations and what they thought they wanted. Then they cried about how their last wives had used and abused them and how they were perfect fathers and providers. After their glory days are over, we get the leftovers... broken-down junky renditions of how they used to be.

June 16, 2006

Lord, I thank you for forgiveness because I need it. I thank you for giving me chance after chance because I needed everyone of them. I'm sorry for my sin; I don't know how I got here so quickly... after rededicating my life to you! Once again, it seems as though I am always sorry about something. I always pride myself on being the best during these summer months. The kids are gone. It is just you and me, God.

I really didn't worry about temptation, but I guess it had to come sooner or later. I have hesitated on writing because I lost my faith, and I did not want to complain or talk to you, God. I had really tried to do what was right, and I felt as if it didn't seem to matter. Then I felt as if I would never find anyone, at least not until the kids graduated. That depressed me. I felt that the last five years of my thirties had been wasted, and I didn't want to be in my forties and not be married. I have frustrated myself to death with this idea.

First, there was the crazy lady who told me that God was going to restore me and Shawn; then there was Derrick, the husband from Hell; then there was Craig.... I have had so much hurt, and I have caused hurt as well. I can't really say where I am going, at this point. I used to love Pre-Paid Legal Legal, but my belief system is now on hold. I can't put it in front of the King.

Chapter Thirteen

September 21, 2006

It has been four months since I last wrote in my journal...a whole season. In that last entry I wrote, I was feeling discouraged and at the end of my rope, emotionally and spiritually. So over the last four months, I didn't want to communicate with God...just a quick bedtime prayer so I could ask God for forgiveness and for Him to watch over my kids and me. No real communication...you see, I lost my faith. My expectations I had for God had not been met. I felt I had no direction and no vision, and without a vision, I thought I would perish. I felt as though it did not matter if I obeyed the rules because I had tried for the last five years, and nobody can be perfect.

When I fell down, I got back up and didn't stay down. I tried to change my approach to sin and shut the world and all of its temptations out for months at a time, only to rejoin the world and have the same temptations staring me in the face...again! Sometimes, I made it through, and sometimes I failed, but nothing I did seemed to move God. I wanted Him to move, tell me something, and give me a clue as to what it is that I am supposed to be doing besides suffering and rewrapping the same wounds that I keep inflicting upon myself. I hated the place I was in. No matter how hard I tried to be a "super saint" or even if I was as weak as water, nothing seemed to change. I convinced myself that I didn't need anyone, and that I was satisfied alone. Wasn't that what single women did when they were about to turn forty?

This all sounds good until the next man comes along and treats me with kindness. Then I begin to justify why I should let this one into my life. We can just be friends, but no! He wants to be friends with benefits. I know this is true, but I think I can convince him to become more. But if a man tells me he just wants to be friends while he is putting his hands all over me, chances are we won't be having a relationship...just the relations part. We women change our minds. That is just what we do, given the right circumstances and words. But a man generally has his mind made up. It's like a woman going into Wal-Mart saying she is going to only buy a gallon of milk. Everything else she sees becomes a necessity, and she comes out with a full shopping cart. But a man...oh, no...he knows what he wants. If he goes into Wal-Mart and says he wants milk, you had better believe he is not going to buy the cow. If his focus is to get some milk, no matter how much we put ourselves on sale, he is not buying. He may go so far as to put us in the shopping cart, but chances are we won't make it to the checkout counter! I guess I needed to recap what I experienced and some of the truths that I learned over my summer.

That had to be the most discouraging time in my entire life to this point. Even before I married Shawn I had known great sorrow beyond believe. If I had started this book back 10 years earlier, I don't think that anyone could bear to read through that much depression. So I was familiar with disappointment and loss. But God stepped in and He gave me nine years of prosperity, favor, a good husband that loved me, a good job and my own business. I began to take God for granted and drifted away from Him. I wasn't so far that I couldn't see the shoreline, but I was out far enough that I would be in danger if a storm came, and guess what! It did!

I was caught off guard, and there was nothing I could do about it. I knew God loved me, and I knew I had asked Him to save me. I guess it was time for salvation. God deals with everyone differently, but I believe the things that are affected by the storm are usually the things that mean the most to us. It could be our job, a loved one, or a relationship, or it could possibly be all of these things at once. Only God knows what you are capable of bearing, and He will give us the grace to go through it. It is only when we assume that God will or will not do certain things in our lives that we begin to lose sight of the purpose of God. We don't always know what His purpose is early on, but we can certainly just simply trust that He knows what is best for our lives. There is always going to be that question mark in our minds that asks, "Why, Lord?" and, "What is it that you want from me?"

I still have those moments, but I often think of Joseph and how he spent many years in an Egyptian prison cell even though he was innocent. I'm sure he thought, "Lord, what is going on? Are these the plans that you have for my life? This is nothing like the dream I had that night. How unfair that my brothers go free and unpunished while I – the only one besides my father who truly loved and worshiped you – am locked away in this prison. Why would you do this to me?" He must have cried many tears of loneliness and felt like he had lost many years of his young adult life. The Bible never mentions that he felt this way, but it does say he wept. He hurt, but he never stop serving God and giving Him the glory. But most importantly, he gained the understanding that what the Devil had meant for his harm God meant for his good. Nations were preserved from the pain of one man. Does that have a familiar ring to it? What can God use from your pain?

The story doesn't end here; it is only the beginning of a new chapter in the pages of life because God gives us the things for which we ask Him. I did meet someone, and I felt he was my soul mate. He wasn't perfect, but he was all that I had asked God for. God had mercy on me and allowed me to marry this man. We were so compatible. He was a little older than I, but he was the kindest, sweetest man I have ever known. But where there is blessing, there is also opposition. My purpose had still not been fulfilled for my life; he was just the provision.

Chapter Fourteen

January 3, 2007

Well, it has been about eight months since I have written. I believe it is because God has healed my heart and answered my prayers. I used my journals as an escape from the pain of my divorce; it was my way of airing out my discrepancies, giving God the praise, asking the Lord to answer my prayers, and writing it down when He did. The only reason why I would not write is I did not want to face God or myself. I am a very honest writer, and there was no point in lying on paper. I was not proud of myself this past year. If I were God, I would probably have given up on me. It was a rocky 2005 and 2006; it's funny how this all began because of my failures. I have learned so much about myself and about God's mercy. I thought I had my life and God's plan for me all figured out in 2003-2004, but when things got worse, I felt like I had to start all over...yet again. I guess what I have also learned is we cannot make God give us what we want through good works or through good behavior. Now don't get me wrong...God wants us to obey, but when our actions toward God are for the wrong reason or we obey just to get God to answer our prayers, what happens when He doesn't? That is where I lived for three years.

January 5, 2007

It didn't seem to matter how long my clean streak went on; at the end, I was always disappointed. I really didn't know what to do. I hated it when I failed God; I felt that my chance of happiness was over and that I had made a fatal mistake. At that point, I was ready to give up on trying to be perfect and just to do the best I could.

January 15, 2007

The years began to pile up. It seemed as though, failure after failure, the Devil was trying to wear me down, and eventually he did. But God's love lifted me. "When nothing else could help, love lifted me!" I thank God that He blessed me with a new husband that is tailored just for me. I face new problems as well as old ones posing as new ones. In 2004 or 2005, I would have accepted any problem as long as it had a good man attached to it, but today I have become a little pickier and somewhat spoiled. January 16, 2007

A funny thing happened; God blessed me in spite of my mess. In 2006, I was in no position to ask God for anything. I gave up on holding out until my change came. I was tired of all the disappointments in my life. I figured if I didn't ask God for anything, I wouldn't be disappointed. Therefore, I stopped talking to Him.

This within itself was a clue that I was not praying 100% of the time. If we are only worshipping God to butter Him up 30% of the time, and begging Him for something the other 70% of the time, when we are let down, we don't feel like worshipping, and we stop asking because it feels as if He isn't going to answer our prayers anyway. So we just stop praying. I lost all my faith, and the Bible says, "Without faith, it is impossible to please God." It's not so much about the faith of what God can do; it's more about faith in who God says He is.

January 17, 2007

Thank you, Lord, for a glorious day. I just got off the phone with my beautiful husband. We were praising God for His wonderful acts of kindness, how He blessed us this week, and how God gave us back our tithes that we had sown earlier in the week. He blessed us to be able to have a weekend out of town. All I had asked Wayne for was one weekend a month for us, and he said "yes." It will help me to have something to look forward to because we would have the kids the majority of the other weekends. That weekend alone will help me to not feel so overwhelmed. Thank you, Jesus, for the small miracles that you give.

Wayne and I were newlyweds. We were still trying to work out the weekends with my new step-kids. I had never really been a step-mom before; therefore, it was an emotional challenge for me as well as his daughter. She had written her father a letter that he did not know I read. She talked about how sad she was that he and her mother were not together anymore. I don't think this had been a problem when he was alone, but now that he was with me, it was painful for her. I felt like the enemy in the camp. I could not tell Wayne that I had read the letter she had written him because he would have felt bad for me. You see, marriage does not solve any of our problems; it only takes the place of our old ones. We still need God's grace in our lives; it is just a different type of grace. I had begged God for almost five years to allow me to find a husband, and He had answered.

March 27, 2007

To God be the glory for the things He has done. Tomorrow will mark the five-year anniversary when Shawn walked out of my life and the process began. I told the Lord I wanted to be a writer. He told me, "You will now finish writing that book I assigned to you 20 months ago," so I have been reading in my spring green 2005 journal. It makes me both laugh and cry.

March 28, 2007

God has been merciful to me. I can't believe it has been five years since Shawn left me. I remember Prophetess telling me it would be five years until my life would be totally restored and that I would be healed, etc… I remember yelling at her and saying, "I ain't gonna wait no five years! I will be forty years old!" I was so mad!

Well, yeah, it took five years when it was all said and done. I thank God I'm still standing, and I'm in my right mind…at least I think I am, but not everyone would agree. Loren is 17 now and will be18 this year while Ash will be sweet sixteen. Wow! They were 10 & 12 when Shawn left. What a difference 5 years can make! I am feeling so good that I'm married to my soul mate. I love Wayne so much. He was worth all five years of pain I went through. He completed my list of qualities that I wanted in a mate. It's amazing just looking back and reading about all that God has done for me. It's funny how crisis can come into our lives and explode into a big ordeal, and "poof!" They are gone, and it is on to the next piece of drama! We waste so much energy due to the fear of what might happen if we don't get things our way, not realizing that in five years or even ten years later, the little things that we stressed over, we won't even remember. Memories with friends and family will last a lifetime. The strife is hard to remember, that is, unless we love holding grudges against people. I know that I have held them myself because I didn't want to forgive or to say "I'm sorry!" Well, I pray for my own life in this area.

August 27, 2007

Lord, I give you all the glory and the praise for allowing me to have peace. It comes in different shapes and forms but mostly in the form of surrender. It has been a rough week…

I didn't write for three months. Wayne and I had a lot of adjusting to do. I stayed busy trying to be a good wife and step-mom as well as a full-time mom. There were days when I questioned God about having gotten married and prayed and asked Him if I had made a mistake again. I missed my two-bedroom apartment and my simple, peaceful life. There had been no one to stress out about, and I did not have to fight over how to raise my kids. I loved Wayne very much, but I don't think I expected it to be this complicated. He had hidden many things from me, especially how attached his daughter was to him. I did not want to be the cause of his or her pain. I began to feel as though he should have stayed single so they could be together without my being in their way. I tell you this not to disrespect my relationship with my husband, but to let you know that when you fall in love or when you are focused on someone and they are focused on you, there comes a point when no one is focusing on God.

God is waiting on us to ask Him His opinion about the situation. I believe if I had slowed down long enough to hear God's voice, He would have said wait a little bit longer so that you can make a decision based on intelligence, not just compatibility and love. But once we have stood before God and man and made those vows, "for better or worse, sickness and in health, richer or poor, to death do us part," it is our responsibility to obey the Lord and to do our very best to stay in God's will because there is peace there that surpasses all understanding.

August 30, 2007

"And poof!" The summer is almost gone. God is so wonderful; He has been so merciful to me. This summer He blessed me with the ministry of dance, and I was also able to build a dance team of girls, including Loren and Ashley. These girls were dead and lifeless when I got them, and now they burst with energy when they praise God. They still struggle with their salvation, but they have come a long way; it is all a process, and it takes time and patience…a lot of patience. Lord, I know I don't deserve to even be in the place that you put me in, but I thank you because I know I could never say to you or myself that I am good enough for ministry. It is just something that I do in spite of my struggles. If we wait until we think the time is right, the Devil will always put drama in our lives. He will have us so preoccupied that we will never have time for God or ministry. Life is a press; we have to keep praying and moving on. If we are stuck on something, it will not only slow us down, but it will begin to eat away at our salvation and our lives.

We all deal with little annoyances; it feels sometimes as if we can't control them. They could drive us crazy. When we try to stop them or focus on controlling them, we take our focus off God, and the Devil has us right where he intended us to be all along…confused and not praying. I dealt with that this week. My husband and I had an argument about his daughter coming down this week, and he hung up on me. My flesh said, "Call him right back and argue with him and hang up on him!" but I heard the Holy Spirit breaking me down to tears and telling me to just walk away and pray.

There is nothing we can do that is more effective than prayer; it is better to put things in God's hands and take hold of God's peace than to fight a battle that we cannot win and still have no peace.

And so I obeyed and prayed. About an hour later, he called me back and apologized. I could hear God saying, "Trust me," but it's hard to trust God and be in control at the same time. Lord knows, I'm a control freak. I hate being out of control with my emotions, my house, my finances, and my life. If God were not in control, it would not be long before I blew it. Then I would be running to Jesus to fix it.

Chapter Fifteen

December 19, 2007

Wow! This year is about over! To God be the glory, we made it one year. Lord, I thank you. You have blessed me so much this year, in spite of my mistakes. I have been married a year, and the walls of obstacles are beginning to crumble.

I talked to Beth today. It has been five years. God is true to his promises; when He restores, He does it fully. Now, I have to learn to forgive and trust again. She really hurt me to my soul...Beth, Prophetess, and Shawn. Well, I don't blame Shawn for leaving because I didn't always do right by him, but it was how and why he left. I was angry because of his lying; he wanted to make people believe that he was not responsible for any of our problems and that he had been this perfect dad. If that were true, then there was no need for him to go around telling people. They would see it for themselves. He knew he had been just as guilty but for different reasons. He had not changed! Anyway, God was going to help me look past all that and forgive him even though Shawn had never said he was sorry for anything. It was hard for me to forgive because of the fact that there never had been a point of closure for that part of my life.

This was my last entry for almost a year. Beth had been my best friend since the 7th grade. We had a misunderstanding that turned into an ugly fight that I hadn't wanted. She did something that friends don't do: She betrayed my trust. I had so many hurts and betrayals; some were well deserved, but some were outright attacks from the enemy. Nevertheless, God was making restitution for all of my wrongs, and he was bringing me closure in certain areas of my past. Still, other areas would take longer to heal. God is so mindful of us that He takes us from "faith to faith" and "glory to glory."

The year of 2008 had been a devastating year for me personally, yet Wayne and I were so happy. I was fired from my job at Chrysler after working there for fifteen years because I decided to allow my friend to clock me out instead of staying there all day. To some of us, it was no big deal. We would take turns leaving early. God warned me to stop, but I did not listen. Shortly after I had lost my job, my mother suggested that I go with her to see a minister that did not claim to be a prophet, but who allowed God to use him. Because of my past, I really didn't like the idea of going to see a prophet, but I wasn't going to let her go alone. Wayne went along, too.

We decided to go in with Mom, and the minister began to speak about my losing my job. He said that the Lord said for me to "stand still and see the salvation of the Lord." He also told Wayne some things that blew his mind, things that were true concerning a close friend of Wayne's. He went on to say that God was taking people out suddenly, and that he needed to get things right. He said God was sending warnings, but people were not taking Him seriously and that God was not playing. When we left, I pondered all that he had spoken to us as well as to my mother. I went home and began to cry out to God for direction, and I asked God to draw me closer to Him. I also asked for forgiveness for what I had done. At that point, He had my full cooperation.

I didn't hear back from Chrysler all summer. Wayne and I had a wonderful summer. We went on weekends to get away, and I got an opportunity to be the stay-at-home wife I had always wanted to be. We grew closer, and I prayed for him every day.

Wayne was addicted to cigarettes. When we met, he said he had quit and that he was saved. He had been raised in the church, and his family members were lifelong members of Christ Church Apostolic. He was perfect in every way except for that. Before long, he was back to smoking, but he was hiding it from me. I have a strong sense of smell, so I confronted him about it. He confessed and said he had tried to stop, but could not stop. I remember one morning standing in front of my big picture window, praying and asking God to completely save him, and the Lord spoke back to me, "No matter what it costs?"

I said, "Yes, Lord, but please don't make him suffer. I love him so much."

I had not yet gotten over the guilt of marrying Wayne. I felt God was going to punish me for marrying Wayne because Wayne smoked and was not perfect. I believed he was saved, but the fact that he was smoking made me nervous and unsure. I lived with this fear always in the back of my mind. I would say to myself, "Any day now, the axe is going to drop. I am finally happy, and this is too good to be true."

The summer wore on into fall, and the season was changing. Wayne was working two jobs to make up for my not working, and so I did my best to make sure he had all the comforts of home at his disposal. I laid out his clothes, fixed him a nice meal for lunch, and fixed him a lunch box for his evening shift job.

Chapter Sixteen

It was now mid-November. I was growing weary about getting my job back at Chrysler. This great sense of depression came over me; I could not seem to shake it for three days. I felt as though I was in mourning, but for what I didn't know. The third day, when Wayne came home from work, he decided to cut the grass. I was upset with him because I knew he had just gotten off work and that he needed to rest.

I went out to help him pick up apples that had fallen from our apple tree off the ground. Afterwards, we went in, and I fixed him lunch. We ate, and he showered and got ready for bed. We lay in the bed, talked, and giggled about the funny events of the day. He told me he loved me so much, and I told him I loved him, too. He reached over to touch me, and I giggled because I knew how tired he was. He looked at me, laughed as well, and said playfully, "Forget you, Lori!"

I told him to go to sleep. I lay there with him as he fell asleep. He rolled over, pulled me close to him, and told me, "Don't leave me, Lori!"

I assured him, "I won't." I lay there for an hour, but I was not asleep.

He would always tell me, "I can't fall asleep unless you're here." It was four o'clock in the afternoon, and I could hear the girls coming in, so I got up and went downstairs to greet them. We had dinner as usual, and then the girls did their homework.

Wayne was off work that night, so I decided to let him sleep through the rest of the night. I had a room downstairs, one in which I could usually write and relax without disturbing him while he slept all evening since he worked the night shift. After dinner, I went into the spare bedroom to lie down and watch TV. Many times, Wayne would only sleep for six hours and then get up, but I was extra quiet so that he would not wake up.

For some reason I felt an overwhelming sense of depression. I had felt that way for three days straight, but I didn't understand why. This night was not any different, and it wasn't just that I didn't feel like doing anything but lying around. I wasn't sleepy, so I began to pray and ask God what was wrong with me, but I understand now. God was preparing me for the most dramatic season of my life. I stayed downstairs until about three o'clock in the morning; finally, I drag myself up the stairs and slipped into bed with my husband. I snuggled up behind him and smelled that familiar smell that I loved so much.

The next morning, I was awakened by the sound of my name being called by my husband. I was startled because it was so early in the morning, and Wayne did not yell my name unless something was wrong. I jumped up and responded to him; he told me it was his blood pressure.

I frantically inquired, "Do you want me to call 911?"

Without waiting for a "yes" response from him, I grabbed the phone and called. While I was on the phone with the dispatcher, he went into a full-blown heart attack. I tried to listen carefully to the dispatcher and do exactly what he was instructing me to do: I was instructed to place Wayne on the floor.

As I attempted to do this, his foot caught in the blanket, but God gave me this super strength to actually pull him up over the covers and onto the floor. I began to call on Jesus in the midst of giving him CPR. The ambulance arrived 15 minutes later. The paramedics had gotten lost because the cable company had not changed our address in the system. It's funny how someone's simply not doing his or her job can mean the difference between life and death.

Out of respect for Wayne's family members that truly loved him, this is where I bring these events to a close.

Wayne's family and I spent four days in the hospital. It was a continuous battle for his soul; he was in a coma. Up to this point, I had never in my life fought such a spiritual battle. I remember when I was in the hospital chapel, I told the Lord, "No matter what happens, I will continue to serve you," and that I would never be the same. At that moment, everything that I had ever known about God changed. I was in all the way. Come life or death, I didn't care! I was going to serve God.

The shock of disbelief and horror gripped my heart and soul, and my mind flashed back to all the disappointments of my past; however, I didn't ask God why. Somewhere in my heart, I already understood why. I remember having had a specific conversation with my cousin Tina. I had told her I was too scared to ask God for what I really wanted...for Wayne to live. Instead, I asked for God's will to be done because I did not think I could take another disappointment from God.

Tina kept telling me, "Ask God for what you want, Lori!"

I told her I was too scared to jump off that cliff. I asked her, "What if I jump off that cliff, and he dies? I don't think I could bare another disappointment!"

She assured me, "If you jump, God will catch you either way. She and I prayed every night for four days straight, in spite of the enemy's constant attacks on me.

On day three, a minister by the name of Damon McCloud came to visit Wayne and me at the hospital; he spoke of Wayne as a butterfly in a cocoon and said that God had told him He was working on Wayne. He also said when God was finished with Wayne, he would be a butterfly. And so I believed God for Wayne's healing.

While I was there, I played Wayne's favorite song, "I'm Still Here." I whispered in his ear, "I'm right here, Baby, and I love you!" I rubbed his legs and feet with lotion and anointed him with Holy Oil. It was the fragrance of myrrh. I thought about how Mary must have felt when she anointed Jesus' body and how much she loved Him, but my pain couldn't even compare to the greatness of hers nor God's for their Son. Wayne's body was so warm and had a beautiful cinnamon glow to it. I then purposely kissed him on his head, hands, and legs because I wanted to remember him forever. On the fourth day, I decided to let go. The doctors said there was nothing else that they could do for him.

PART FOUR: RESTORATION

Chapter Seventeen

November 30, 2008

This is first time that I have written in a year. My husband Wayne has been gone now for 12 days. I thought I would die along with him when he was in the hospital those four days. Actually, it is more difficult to write this than it is to pretend he didn't die. When I journal, it takes me to another world, not exactly the one I want to be in. It is a place of realization, and it is very real here. If I had it my way, I wouldn't stay here long, but I understand there is purpose behind my pain.

Tomorrow, if Wayne had lived, we would be celebrating our 2nd anniversary. He died nine days before my birthday and thirteen days before our anniversary. I went to my nephew's church today. The service was good. I went up for prayer and gave my request. I told the man of God I wanted God to return to me the things that had been taken from me and to continue to give me peace.

There is one thing at which I marvel. When I was at the hospital, I thought I was going to lose my mind! The scripture that said, "We fight not against flesh and blood but the principalities and the rulers of darkness" was right on the money! I had never before seen attacks that were so shameless…getting "cussed out" by my husband's ex-in-laws, people sneaking in the room at one o'clock in the morning and disrespecting my brother-in-law Reggie. I can't believe some of the things his family said: for example, I had dragged out Wayne's recovery time eight hours too long and "If it were my husband, I would have pulled the plug. It's over, and we need to get back to our lives!" Wayne would have been devastated by the way some of the people who claimed to love him had acted! The last time I checked, love was patient, kind, longsuffering, did not become easily angered.…

If they had truly loved him, they would have protected me, not hurt me. That is why God had to explain to us not to take it personally when people hurt us. The more love we have, the fewer devils we have, which, in return, will help us to treat people kind, even when they are nasty to us. I pray that God heals my heart in that area. They hurt me worse than the pain of Wayne's death. The sad thing about it is that, without a doubt, everyone is going to have to go through the death of a loved one and deal with family, whether it be theirs or their in-laws, and the Bible says, "Do not be deceived, God is not mocked; for whatever a man sows, this he will also reap." Woe to those who were just plain mean! Now that I have gotten this written down on paper, I am going to try to let it go and attempt to forgive…yet again.

Wayne passed away November 18, 2008. I decided to take a road trip to Birmingham, AL, to see my friend Mary. While I was down there, Mary and I took a trip to Atlanta. I felt this was necessary to explain, because my journals are sometimes hard to follow.I have never liked the idea of a long recovery, even though it seems I was always in recovery from something. I felt that writing Wayne a letter would help me to say good-bye, and it did. During the time, he was in the hospital I had two choices. On one hand, I could cry and ask God why; on the other hand, I could grab hold to the hem of His garment and not let go in spite of the outcome. There is healing in the hem of His garment; to this day, I have never let go. I chose not to do a lot of writing between my journal entries. This book is a nine-month's journey in comparison to an actual seven-year's journey. Watch how quickly God can restore your life when your will is aligned with His purpose for your life. I had made up my mind in that chapel at the hospital that I would never be the same, and I meant it. This time around, I was going to see my way through, all the way to the other side or this trial, come Hell or high water. I was not going to give up or give in.

What I am about to tell you is not meant to disrespect my husband in any way, it is for the sole purpose of God's glory. My husband did not get the insurance money switched over to my name after we married. I do not believe he intentionally did this. No one expects to die at fifty-one years old.

Shortly after he died, I received a phone call and was told that I was penniless. I was once again left with a shattered heart, two teen-age girls, no employment, and a $1000.00 a month rent payment. Both of my daughters were seniors in high school and would be graduating in the spring. In addition to that, I had a car note and utilities.

Hint: When you are down to nothing, God is always up to something!

Chapter Eighteen

January 23, 2009

I'm in Birmingham, Alabama, visiting my friend Mary, and, Lord, I thank you for allowing me to take this trip and for allowing me to safely make it here without any problems. Mary, her sister, and a few other friends went with me to dinner tonight. I was glad to be able to share with them about the loss of my husband and your mercy and kindness to me. One lady commented that it has to be God because I should be a zombie right now. I told her I stay in the Word constantly and that Joyce Meyers and I are as best friends, I listen to her every day. I really enjoyed being able to share the Word of God with others. It was therapy for me.

January 24, 2009

I felt like dying today. I was in a busy mall full of people, yet I felt so alone. I miss Wayne so much. Mary asked if I was O.K. I told her the truth, that I missed him. She didn't say much. I think it's hard for her to understand how I feel because it had hurt her feelings that I got married, and didn't tell her before I did. Nevertheless, it was a miserable day for me, watching couples go by...young and old, gay and straight. (We were in Atlanta!) I decided since I missed

Wayne, I would write to him so I could at least talk to him, even though I realize he couldn't talk back.

"*Dear Sweetheart,*

It has now been two months since my nightmare began. I relive that Friday morning in my head everyday. It is like a bad movie that is on every channel, one you can't turn off. It's warm here in the South; it reminds me of fishing weather. I can't believe you're not here with me. The last thing you said to me the night before you died was, 'Don't leave me, Lori,' and then you turned around and left me here. I have a million 'if onlys' to say to you. My favorite one is 'if only you had not smoked' or 'if only I had made you quit.' I still love you in spite of the fact that I just wish you could have lived your life with more purpose. I miss your funny smile; I miss us laughing until we fell asleep; I miss our inside jokes. There are so many habits I picked up from you that will always remain with me, such as making my bed up every single day. I'm afraid if I don't, I will get out of the good habit you got me into. I consider you every day. I say the funny stuff that you would say, and I find others laughing at it, too. You were truly the love of my life. I can't go by a lake, and not smile and think 'are there any fish in there?' No one will ever take that from me. People will come and try to replace you, but your love will never be matched...not this love. It may come, but it will be different. I loved you without reservation. It was a free fall love, even when in my heart knew that something was going to happen to us. I always knew the ax was going to fall because I was finally happy. Until I met you, happiness always ran from me. I know you felt the same way. I could feel it in your kisses and hugs...even in the way you stared at me when you didn't think I was aware of your watching me. Baby, I hated to see you go, but I love you enough to understand why it was best that you did. No more child support, or people calling you to paint or fix this and that, or to pour their problems out on you.

To use you for whatever they could get from you, or to even hurt you because they were miserable with their own lives, and hated to see you get a little bit of joy out of your life. Baby, I am glad you're at rest. I'm glad you're with your dad. I know how much you missed him. Now you can fish on the most incredible lakes that ever existed, and hunt on the most beautiful land that God has ever created. You are free from stress and money, bills and rent. I can't wait to see you again, but I guess I will have to.

Wayne, I'm not mad about the money anymore. I understand that God has the last say-so in the plans for my life. What the Devil meant for evil, God meant for my good. God is taking care of me. I know now that he meant it to be that way. Thank you for taking care of me the two years that you did. You were never selfish and gave me everything you had. Thank you for trusting me to take care of our business, and I did. We had a great life, didn't we? We went on so many adventures both in the woods and in the city. Thank you for showing me places that I didn't even know existed, and I'm glad I did the same for you (Bruno's Pizza). I'm going to say good bye for now, but not forever. I love you, Baby.

Love always, Lori

Lord, I thank you for a safe trip to Atlanta and back. Today was quite different from last night. I was tired from all the shopping I had done yesterday. I didn't get any Word today. I have to have the Word of God everyday, or I cannot function.

Thank you, Lord, for my life. I thank you for being in my right mind two days before Valentine's Day. To tell the truth, I dreaded its coming. I was not sure how I was going to handle it this time. But God stepped in and super-charged my heart; I have been filling my heart with the Word of God. What a difference the Word of God makes!

April 1, 2009

Wow! I can't believe it is April already! I promised the Lord I would write today! It has been almost two months since I have written. I have been working on my book. <u>Why Do You Cry?</u> I certainly know why I do! I guess it is everyone's journey with God to find out why they do as well. Once I found out, I didn't stop crying. It's just that I now understood that there is a purpose for my tears. What is your purpose? Is it to help a child that has been sexually abused, or to counsel a forty-something year old wife whose husband tells her he doesn't love her anymore after being married for twenty-four years, or even to comfort a friend who just lost a job...or even worse, her husband. All of these incidents are real, but so is God's love and kindness. We have to understand that our tears are painful and real, but they are only temporary. I don't mind crying if I know it's going to cause others to become healed. No one understands this better than Jesus does.

Every month God has taken me a little farther than I ever thought I could go. My friends and family are waiting for me to fall apart, but God continues to hold me up. I cry everyday, but my tears are for Jesus; I pour out all of my emotions while worshiping. I balled my eyes out today, but I let the Lord know that these tears were tears of surrender and worship. I worship God for my loss and for each tear that drops from my eyes. I cannot imagine crying for days and giving all of my tears to a piece of tissue that can only catch them, but God says he bottles up my tears. I find great comfort in knowing that, and in also knowing that my tears will someday be replaced with joy because I trusted in Jesus, not in what a man could do for me.

This time around is so different from when I wrote about Shawn leaving me seven years ago. I didn't know Jesus like I do now. I can't really say I know what my future holds, but I will say I trust Him completely. This trust takes away the crazy guesswork of trying to figure out what God is going to do. I guess that is the major difference. I could never figure out what the end was going to be, so I would conjure up my own ending and had the nerve to be upset if God did not follow my expectations. It is safe to say, "God, I trust you" is the most intelligent response that we can ever give to God.

April 2, 2009

I want to give God all the glory and the praise for waking me up this morning because He is worthy of at least a "thank you" and so much more. I shied away from writing in my journal not only because of school, and because of writing the book, but because I didn't want to feel the depression that sometimes accompanies writing after a loss. However, I am gratefully surprised! I don't know why? God always lifts me up. I guess I felt like avoiding the very thing that God wanted me to do. As I was writing my book and got to Part Three, I suddenly felt it was coming to an end, and I have not yet received my promises from God. I began to pray to God and ask Him, "How is this supposed to help anyone when I am still waiting on you to fulfill your promises to me?"

The Lord began to encourage me to continue to write in my journal. There is so much more to come. It never stops being a faith walk, no matter how far we have come. I used to think I had the power to make things happen; I would use all of my effort to kick down doors as if I was Wonder Woman, but God did not get any glory for what I did. It doesn't mean I should lie down and do nothing, but it's about having faith, regardless of what God decides for my life, I will be in total agreement with Him, even if I don't know what His plans are for my life.

"Lord, I trust you." I find myself saying that at least every two hours, especially when someone hurts my feelings or when I have yet another door slammed in my face. I have had so many "no's" in the past year that they are too many to count, but every time the sting of the word "no" hits my heart, I just began to say, "Lord, I trust you," and I will continue to say it until my change comes…or the Rapture, whichever comes first.

God does know what He is doing, even though I feel as though He has forgotten me. Sometimes, He can be so quiet, and I can feel so alone. I have learned to get in His presence and just worship with my tears…not complain or have a pity party…but just worship. How can He not hear me? He is teaching me perseverance, in spite of how it looks. God's Word cannot lie. If He says, "I will never leave you or forsake you," that is what he means. I may feel forsaken at that moment, but I'm not because God cannot lie, so I have to be wrong. That is why the Bible says, "Lean not unto your own understanding, but in all of thy ways acknowledge Him and He will direct your path." This is not a feeling walk, but a faith walk.

I find myself constantly reviewing the things that I have written, and I have to eat them for breakfast, lunch, and dinner. How can I write things that I don't always believe? That would make me a hypocrite, now wouldn't it? So when I become discouraged, I have to encourage myself. God will hold me accountable for anything I write that is a lie. Therefore, I have to follow my own advice, and I have to realize the things that I write are not only for others but to help encourage me. As a woman, it's easy to talk strong in front of my girlfriends, telling them what I won't put up with, and so on, but when I write it down, and it's my turn to go though the test, can I stand to take all that wise advise that I have preached to my friends? That is where I am now. I have to live it.

I have situations in my life that arise and catch me off guard, and God brings me right back to the place where I said, "Can you walk away from what is not good for you? Can you hear God telling you 'no' and obey Him?" Not only do I have to write it, but I have to be able to live it; otherwise, my book would be yet another pointless book wherein a woman is only glorifying herself and giving others no hope that they can ever be free from their struggles. I now understand that I don't have to be a super saint to walk with God. I just have to be an obedient one.

April 3, 2009

God, I thank you in advance for the things you're going to do, and for my future. It has not been easy these last few days. I believe once a month God pulls away and allows me to see things from a real point of view. If He wasn't keeping me and shielding me from all the pain that is due to me, I would lose my mind. I couldn't carry this load for even five seconds. I don't think I see what others perceive. That is why I get the look of pity from so many people... or they think I'm in denial...or crazy, but I know it is God carrying my cross for me just as He carried the sins of the world on His own Cross. Knowing that does not always make it easier in my mind, but my heart bleeds for the pain I know Jesus must have felt. I can't even bare my tiny cross for five minutes without balling my eyes out!

During this season in my life, I was obviously still grieving the loss of my husband. However due to not having any income I was dealing with the struggle of not being able to pay my bills. Somehow, every month God interceded and gave me just enough to make it through each month. I felt as though I didn't have time to properly grieve my husband because I was too occupied with my financial situation. Looking back, I believe God meant it to be this way. He is so awesome in the way he works things out for our good.

April 4, 2009

What a mighty God we serve! God's greatness is not based on the answering of my prayers. I have prayed many prayers that have not been yet answered. His greatness is based upon His Word. I cried all day today, unlike I have done since Wayne died. I questioned the Lord about when it is going to get better. I felt as though I wanted to just give up and not fight anymore. It's not that I didn't want to serve God. I just felt as if I had no more strength to fight my battles and everyone else's, too! I just wanted to lie down and wait for God to pick me up, and if He didn't, then I would just have to perish. I am all out of everything…strength, money, but not faith. I never run out of faith; it is the time frame that makes my life so hard to bear. The silence of Wayne not being here, and the fear of my girls' growing up and leaving me alone. I just knew Wayne and I would retire and live out our days on the water fishing, and now I am afraid to plan anything because it hasn't worked out for me in the past.

I'm waiting on a change, but I have no idea of what I'm waiting for. I watched the Hallmark channel. There was a Christian Series on all day. I'd say there were six movies in a row, and in all of them, somebody's husband died…all six of them…and at the beginning and at the end, I heard a familiar scripture: "To everything there is a season, and a time to every purpose under the sun, a time to be born and a time to die; a time to plant and a time of harvest." (Ecclesiastes

3:1) I have finally gotten my answer; my season of planting is not yet over, and my season of mourning is not yet over.

This is why I love the Word of God so much. God is never silent in His Word. I felt that at times He had ignored my pain and allowed my suffering to go on longer than I would have liked, but at the end of the day, He did answer through His Word or sometimes through a phone call from a relative or friend or even like my case today though a simple movie. It's been a long day, but I do feel renewed.

April 14, 2009

Happy birthday, Mom! My mother is 68 years old. I'm so grateful that she is still alive and in good health. I am so proud of her and both my step-dad and my natural dad. They have all done a marvelous job of taking care of themselves. They are wonderful examples. I have never in my life seen my dad smoke, curse, or drink, nor have I seen my mom smoke or drink. When I was a little girl, I remember reading her lips when she accidentally slipped, while she was stepping off a curb, and she said the "S" word. I asked her when she got in the car if she had said it, and she laughed and willingly admitted to her sin. We laugh about it to this day.

Lord, I thank you for this day. My PMS week was quite emotional. I believe it was an attack from the enemy because I had shared the Bill Wiese "23 minutes in Hell" testimony with so many people the week before. But I still thank you, God, for the blood. It covers us when we are weak. The joy of the Lord is my strength! He has pulled me out of the pity party and renewed my faith once more. I often have to remind myself that it has to be this way. How can I tell others, "I know how you feel," if I have never felt hopeless myself? When I do feel that sense of hopelessness, it is so real in my mind. It's crazy how the enemy can bring us to a low point of disbelief in such a short period. It reminds me of the prophet Elijah. I used to be so critical of that scripture and think how could he not believe that God would protect him after such a great victory, moments earlier. But now I understand, "The weapons of our warfare are not carnal, but mighty through God,"

It was never Elijah. It was always God's power working through Elijah. And when the power of God was not operating, it was just Elijah alone, with nothing but his thoughts of insecurity...just like the rest of us. Even though I hate the road that I have to travel sometimes, when I hear great testimonies of what God did for others, and how He brought them through, I become jealous because I want my own testimony and I want to share the greatness of God's mercy in my life, too! There is just the part in between that really isn't so glamorous, but I know that someday when I look back on my life, this part...you know the part that really sucks...is the only part that will be the healing balm for someone else's life.

I saw my brother-in-law today. I felt as though God given me a little piece of Wayne back through him. He made me laugh for two hours straight. I hadn't laughed like that since the day before Wayne had his heart attack. He is so much like Wayne, even his hands. He was probably wondering why I was staring at his hands. I couldn't help it! I just needed to see Wayne's gentle hands again, and I did. Reggie, they call him "Wimp," has been such a wonderful brother to me. He makes me laugh, and he encourages me to go on. He does not sugarcoat the fact that some of his family has treated me unfairly. He also assures me that Wayne loved me, even though I still cannot fully understand why he had left me the way he did.

I thank God because He knows whom to send, and He knows how to mend a shattered, not broken, heart. Shattered implies that the pieces cannot be put back together – but God can, and He is doing that for me! Every day I grow a little stronger. The more I listen to the Word of God, the less I can hear the discouraging words of the enemy telling me that I will never get out of this mess, I will never have any money, I won't get my job back, and my kids will not have a good graduation and it all my fault. However, I hear God saying, "For we know that all thinks work together for the good of those who love the Lord," and that He would not put more on us than we can bear, as well as "In due season if we faint not, we shall reap a harvest!"

God cannot lie! My circumstances are a part of God's divine plan for my life, and I choose to trust Him. Even when I'm sad and crying, I trust Him. I love God so much! I don't have any other choice but to trust Him. There are no other options but to trust Him. Where could I go to find the right answer but to Him? I have traveled many roads in my life, and when I was done playing "patty cake" with the Devil, God was right there saying, "Are you done playing? Now it's time for you to get back to business!" There is no escaping the call of God on my life. It is either God's way or our own way to destruction that will take us straight to Hell. If you have ever asked God to save you at anytime in your life, He is going to honor your request, and, yes, it sometimes hurts, but in the end, it will be worth it all!

Chapter Nineteen

April 28, 2009

It has been two weeks since I last wrote. The time seems to go by so quickly. I started on a 21- day fast, and I am on my last leg of the fast. Lord, I want to thank you for so many miracles that I didn't give you credit for on these last few weeks. First, my dad brought me a brand new lawn mower when I did not have one. Then Loren's car went out…at least we thought it did…and it was only out of gas. Thank you, Jesus! Then my microwave blew up, and I didn't get upset. That right there is praise in itself! My mom was supposed to bring me an old one she had. When she told me to get it out of the trunk of her car, I did. It was brand new! God is so faithful!

Sometime in April, Craig had called me out of the blue. He told me he was in the hospital, but he would not tell me why. I had a bad feeling about going to see him at that time, nor did I want to visit a hospital so soon after my ordeal with Wayne. I called my cousin Natalie to ask her opinion about going to visit him, I felt guilty about not going. I guess I needed her to ease my conscience about my choice. I had no idea what Craig was facing; however, later I would find out.

Cont…I talked to my cousin Natalie last week. I really needed a word from God. I asked her about Craig because he had asked me if I would like to go to the movies sometime. I felt as though God was saying "no" because prior to that, the Lord had stopped me from going to visit him in the hospital. I felt afraid to even call him – but I did – to tell him I wouldn't be coming to visit. I felt so bad because my nature is to help those whom I care about. Natalie told me the Lord had said go on with my life. I wasn't sure of what she meant, so she made it plain to me, "Uh… that was a 'No.'" At this time in my life, God wanted my full attention.

May 1, 2009

Thank you, Lord, for keeping me sane another month. It has been one year and three months since I have worked. The Lord used Wayne to take care of me the first year, and He is taking care of me now. I don't want to sound as though I don't worry because I do, I am a very independent person. I remember feeling this way back in 1989 when I was on Welfare and going to beauty college. The difference was that I did not depend on God, and I resorted to my own devices to make ends meet. But when God saves us and He is in control, there is no more lying and cheating to get by. It is a clean road, and it is a narrow road. God leaves us without an excuse. There is no reason to sin no matter how desperate we feel, and I feel really desperate right now. I asked God why? Why did it have to take so long? "Don't you see me falling apart? It's one day before my girls' prom, and 30 days until they graduate from high school? I still don't have a job, and I don't have any savings. I spent it on my rent…no more cushion." It's just God and me.

I needed to write this down because I have to let others know that I have felt strong after church service, and three hours later, angry at the preacher on T.V. because his ABC and 123 steps to financial freedom didn't seem to be working for me. I have sown hundreds of dollars, even when I knew I had bills due and that was all I had, and I'm still waiting for my blessing.

I don't think God will be mad because I wrote this down. He knows my thoughts anyway. I really can't say that I fully understand why He chose to take me around the backside of the mountain, but as I write at this moment, I am watching TBN. A young woman came on and began to talk about the death of her sister's husband and why God took her the long way around. And now she was singing a song about asking God why, He had allowed her husband to die after she had prayed and had done everything she knew to do. The rest of the song said, "I can question God, or I can choose to trust Him." It is as if God is answering me even as I write here and now. It is the message I have longed to hear.

I am getting so frustrated with trying to do everything right so that my trials will be over sooner because there is so much pain here, but the pain is the fire that is making me into a clean vessel that God can use someday. The more I write, the clearer things become. I will have to remind myself again tomorrow to choose to trust God. This is my dark moment, but my time is coming when the sun will shine again. I heard this young lady say that trials are a part of life. It isn't like I didn't know that. However, with the lost of my job, Wayne's dying in my arms, and the cruelty of his family to me at the hospital, and all the pain – it seemed that God would rush in and rescue me!

Come to find out, the very people who were against me got all his insurance money. That is why I had held on so strongly…because I thought it wouldn't be long until God would avenge me and set things right. Now that months have gone by and the friends and family have gone back to their lives with their good jobs, I sit here trying to do everything the preacher says to get out of this lonely, broken place I live in, because it hurts so badly, and I had only counted on being here for a short stay. I only mustered up enough courage to be here a short term; I was truly "waiting to exhale" from this nightmare of a trial.

However, now I am beginning to see this not as a trial. It is God's way of molding me and making me. It has nothing to do with my fasting or my performance. It is just choosing to trust God for that day. I am slowly giving over to my old ways of thinking; I guess all I have to go on are the past references of my Christian walk. I want to say I have been in this place before, and God saw me through, but for some reason my mind blocks out the positive things that God has done, and the Devil whispers in my ear, "You have to be perfect in order for God to help you," and then he says, "Didn't you do everything right, and God still hasn't delivered you? Now what are you going to do?" But I'm so glad that God's Word comes in and stabilizes my mind. I realize that I am so messed up without God's grace and mercy, and even though it is an every moment battle to keep my faith, I have learned to do battle in that way. I have tried really hard to not get mad at God for not interceding the way I thought He should have months ago, but I have the common sense to know my help comes from God and God alone. My thoughts are not even close to His thoughts, and my ways are certainly not His ways. The big picture is what He sees; however, God's delivering me is all I want, because the pressure of not having enough money is driving me insane! For some reason, every day I wake up in my right mind. Thank you, Jesus, nothing has been shut off. I still have my home and food in my cabinets and, more importantly, the love and protection of God over my life and my kids. When I add it all up, I have to acknowledge that God always knows what is best for me. There are things that God has not revealed to me about my "whys."

When He does brings me out, I don't want to be ashamed for the way I acted while I was in, so I say please forgive me, gracious Father, and help my unbelief.

What you just read was an actual battle of my mind. It was important to show how Satan comes into our thought-life. He is relentless; he never takes a break. It is his desire to destroy our minds with doubt and fear. I realize this part of the book is rather uncomfortable for those who have never struggled with a great loss. However, it is my desire for those who are going through a great loss to gain comfort in knowing that they are not alone. The emotions that are felt are real; nevertheless, God said He would never leave you nor forsake you. The best defense against the enemy is the Word of God.

May 3, 2009

Lord, I'm smiling at you right now. God, I thank you for allowing me to see the movie <u>The Color Purple</u> for the first time. I know it came out in 1985, but at that time, we were not allowed to go to the movies, and at the age of nineteen years old, I can't say that I would have wanted to go to the movies to see it anyway. People have always asked me why I hadn't seen it. I could only say I don't know. It was always in the middle when I found it on T.V., and I wanted to see it from the beginning. I have always been a movie lover, especially of movies that were Oscar winners of the eighties. I was too young to appreciate the true meaning of them then, but I knew people made a big fuss about their being so deep and full of wisdom.

Well, Lord, <u>The Color Purple</u> had me in tears. I thought about the two sisters and how much they needed each other. It reminded me of Loren and Ashley. Then I thought about how they suffered, but God gave Ceely her sister Netty back only to have her sister *thrown out by her abusive husband. The separation from Ceely at that time broke her heart, and I'm sure she lost her faith in God for taking away the only little bit of happiness she had. But what she didn't see was that God was working behind the scenes and was using her sister to keep contact with her lost children. Toward the end of the story when Ceely's step-dad died, she realized that she was the rightful heir of the land, house, and the store because it belonged to her father. It had always been hers; she just didn't know it. She was so used to being told that she was nothing and useless that she believed the lies. But God knew all along that it belonged to her, and no matter how long it took, she would receive her inheritance. At the end of the story, her old, rotten husband had to do right by her, and he did. He looked on in the distance as Ceely and Netty were reunited, and God gave her back everything she thought she had lost. God prepared a table in the presence of her enemies. I love the song "Maybe God Is Trying to Tell You Something." I cried the last half hour of the movie. It was a wonderful depiction of how God works for the good in our lives.*

May 10, 2009

Dear Lord, I thank you for another Mother's Day. It was nice. I spent it with my mother and my sisters and brothers. I am so grateful that I have a mother.

May 10, 2009

I just got home from seeing T.D. Jakes. It was so good. He reaffirmed what God has been saying to me all along, which is to worship and not to worry. Today was the last day of my unemployment. I was caught off guard, but I began to sing, "Cry your last tear! It's is going to be all right." I have to choose God, because He is my source. Things are as dark as they can get, but, I still believe God, or I will die trying!!!

I am in so deep with God. It's sort of like when you fall in love with someone. Even when things don't go so well, you look beyond what you see to what you believe that it will be. You believe the promises that the person you fell in love with made to you. That is how I feel about God. He told me to trust Him, even though I have been hurt and disappointed many times before, like the night before Wayne died the second time. I believed God for Wayne to come out of the coma, and I prayed for him not to be healed in death but to be healed on this side, but I also prayed that God would save Wayne. The choice was ultimately God's choice. When I decided to pray that prayer, I was so scared to pray for what I wanted. I was afraid that I couldn't bear to be disappointed by God, but I finally choose " to leap off the cliff, and God caught me" and saved my mind from shattering into a million pieces.

Now, here I am with my Job experience (the one in the Bible), the worst Hell I have ever been through, and my heart aches for God to rescue me. He has not delivered me on this side, but I believe it is already done on the other side. It doesn't mean I don't cry or hurt. I do every day, but when I am done, I still choose to believe God and it hurts!!! It hurts to love someone, and he does not respond to me the way I want him to. This is just like a spouse that doesn't give his mate her way when he can clearly see that she is hurting. She won't leave her mate; she just cries and lets him know how much she hurts and that that she loves him. God is now my husband, my Lord as well as the love of my life! I have broken down all of my walls of fear, being hurt and the fiery trials that it takes to get to the next level. I have cried so many tears of unbelief and then had to go back and repent within the next hour, only to have to go through the jungle of analyzing in my mind why the Word of God isn't working out for me the way the preacher said it would.

I have always struggled with that. It was like it worked for the preacher, so what was wrong with me? Why did God's Word say it if it wasn't working for me? I did believe as hard as I could; I even fasted for 19 days straight! I had to get past my hurt and pain of God's not delivering me right away, and the fact I had spoken things into existence or I had fasted and believed God for a miracle. This trip I was taking wasn't just an ordinary trial. This was a fiery trial. This was one of those processes that would change the way I viewed God and the Cross. He was allowing me to feel what He had felt when He had to endure the injustices of life. God did not intervene because His purpose was more important than the pain Jesus had to go though. Even Jesus felt forsaken, so why shouldn't we expect to go through a small amount of the pain that Jesus suffered along with feeling as though God had left Him?

Now that I had accepted the fact that this journal will be read by everyone who reads my book, I felt it was necessary that I share my real thoughts and feelings, including the doubts that caused me to crack at the seams of life. Trials are a part of salvation; they help to strengthen our thought process and to realize what we really think about God when He doesn't move in our time. He is a force to be reckoned with! It is better to just hold our hands up and surrender because that is the beginning of what God is trying to do for us. God's way sometimes takes a long time. It did for Abraham, David, Hannah, Joseph, and especially the children of Israel, and no matter how I feel about waiting, I would rather wait here on earth with God than to turn away from God and wait from a holding cell in Hell, only to have God say, "You couldn't wait for me to deliver you, so now you're lost for eternity!" When I look at it that way, I don't mind waiting on you, Lord.

May 19, 2009

Sweet Father God, I thank you for it has been 6 months since Wayne's transformation up to Heaven. God has given me a new prospective on Wayne's passing. I no longer grieve his passing as a loss, but I count him as being the one who was blessed, because I know that he is with Jesus. When someone dies in the Lord, we really don't grieve for him; we grieve for ourselves because we are the ones left here to experience the loss.

The loved one isn't in Heaven grieving because he can't stay on earth, because "in the presence of God there is fullness and joy." (Psalms 16:11) The loss is still there, but it does not consume me. Jesus is a reality in my life, and He is always present with me. Grief is a normal part of the process, and I still do miss Wayne, but his death is not my source of life. God is and will always be my source; otherwise, I would have died with Wayne. God has commanded me to live because He still has more plans for my life.

If I had not gone though Katrina in 2002, I would not have been able to believe God for the restoration from this destructive storm. I smile and sometimes cry at the storms in my life, but at the end of the day, God has the last laugh. He will do what He promised me way back in 2002... ***"give me an expected end."*** *I still hold God to His Word, because His Word is still good and will not return void. I also have to thank God, for it's been six months because six months ago I was telling God I couldn't wait to get as far away from Wayne's death as possible. There was no way to get away from it, other than to go through it. God has carried me through, and I have no reason to not believe He will continue to walk with me though the promises as well as to manifest the plans He has for my life.*

God has also put Loren Wilcox in my life to encourage me. We are so compatible. I love her strength and bravery at such a young age. There are things that she knows that I have never heard of in God's spiritual realm. She is constantly bringing things to my attention…even those things that I could not have even imagined asking God for. I thank God for her. She is also a blessing to Loren and Ashley. They receive her when she is talking about the Gospel, even more than I could have ever imagined. She is an answer to my prayer when it comes to talking to the girls about the Word of God.

Chapter Twenty

May 26, 2009

Thank God for the Blood! It is the day after Memorial Day. I spent Memorial Day cleaning Wayne's clothes out of the closet. I folded every shirt neatly, as I smiled and remembered where he wore each outfit. Each shirt held a special memory in my heart. I was trying to figure out what he was wearing when we first met. I found that outfit and set it aside for his brother Donald. I figured it would be nice to see his clothes being worn by his brothers and his son D.J. When I was done sorting everything, I called Reggie and asked him to come and pick up the clothes and make sure D.J. got to pick from them first. I thank God for giving me such a peace in my heart as I went through his things. I had put it off several times before. I just wasn't ready then, and really hadn't planned on doing it yesterday, but I felt like God was telling me it was time to move forward, and I felt His presence with me. Only God can do that! He breathed on me all day; He kept the spirit of depression away and gave me peace, but I first had to choose peace instead of pity.

Reggie came over and picked up the clothes. He stayed and talked to me and had me laughing so hard for two hours straight. I gave him all of the family pictures that Wayne had taken from Mama's house. Reggie mentioned that Mama had grieved about her husband's flag, and it so happened that I had it. I gave it to him to give to her. Later on that day, I thought about her grieving the Veteran's flag and thought about how they had given my flag to D.J. and felt the pain that some of Wayne's family had caused me all over again in my heart. I cursed the thought of it, in Jesus' name and began to tell God that I loved Him. I have to constantly ask God to help me to forgive them every time I think about what they had tried to do to me. I say tried because the Devil's intention was to make me lose my mind...but he didn't!... and he tried to cause me to lose everything I had...but he hasn't done that either!

I will get my stuff back because God will never allow the Devil to win in my life. He is the God of restoration, and He is preparing a table in the presence of my enemies. I love Him because I don't have to fight those kinds of battles. "Vengeance is mine," says the Lord. "I will repay!" I hold fast to His Word, because without it, I would be so messed up in my head. There is no telling what I would have done to them or would have said to them. But for the grace of God who is my strong tower, and my psychiatrist, by the time I was done with dealing with everything and everyone, I needed God to be just that. I am a witness He can keep us sane.

May 27, 2009

"And My God shall supply all my needs according to His riches and glory." I thank God for being my provider! Today, I went to Marion to pick up my Financial Aide check from school. The night before I went, I had prepared a letter and some documents for a grant called An Unusual Circumstances Grant. When I got there, God had already set things up for me. The lady who did the paperwork for the grant was there. She took my paperwork and filed it immediately and told me that I would be receiving a $4,000 grant in ten days and another $5,000 grant next month. Look at

God! I cried as she told me, and she hugged me and said, "God is so good!" I felt like a weight had been lifted off of me. God was just in time. The girls would graduate in four days. God had proven Himself to me, personally. Not that this was the first time. He had done this before, but when we go through an intense fiery trial, our faith is shaken to a whole new level.

It is the Devil's job is to make us think that God, for some odd reason, wants us to suffer and that He may not deliver us. The thing with the Devil is he uses what we know to be true about the Word of God, but he distorts it with a slight bit of a lie, just enough to make us doubt the Word of God. Before we realize it, we begin to question the very Word of God. The enemy will suggest that the Word isn't going to work for us because our circumstance is different from what the preacher is talking about. I know this to be true because he made my life a living hell for many months on end. I had to silence him by screaming, "I know God is real, and I trust Him."

June 6, 2009

Praise be to God, my children have finally graduated high school. I never thought I would see this day come! This is the first time I have seen the evidence of working hard at something and it's truly coming to pass. It feels like a dream! My girls are young women now!

June 12, 2009

Praise the Lord! God has done so much for me in such a short time. The Bible says, "And suddenly God came." That is what has happened to me. God is opening doors faster than I can run though them. First, I got nine thousand dollars in grants, and then, God gave me my unemployment back. Then, not more than a couple days following that, God cancelled all of my outstanding debt. I have often asked Him, "What am I supposed to be doing right now?" I felt guilty because I was not working and felt like I needed to be, but God keeps shutting the doors to employment at this time. But He keeps making a way for me to pay my bills every month, and He allows me to have money for the things I need and want. I love Him because He's faithful; I love Him because He shows me, Lori, that He loves me. He has caused me to fall in love with Him, not His hand. God has done this by not giving me every little thing that I cried for and asked for. He took me the long, tender way through the desert of pain and caused me to solely depend upon His grace and mercy. I realized that I had a choice to go my own way, but I had already been down that road, and after twenty years of being in denial that there were consequences to not trusting and obeying God, I told God that I wanted Him to have His way in my life, and that I would not hold anything back from Him. I told God I would give Him everything that was within me and that I wanted all that He had been trying to give me for the last forty-two years. I asked Him to heal me completely, and told Him that I would not substitute a man, T.V., shopping, or anything that would distract me from my healing. There are times when those distractions still come, but God reminds me of what I had asked Him to do, and I again realign my thoughts back to Christ.

I have often found myself admiring those who preach the gospel of Christ. What did it take for them to get to that place in God? We cannot always see the middle part of their struggles, only the finished product. It leaves us with the question, will we ever get there?

This is my middle part, this is the part that is not glamorous, yet it is where one can be the closest to the Father. Where there is no pain, there is no glory. For those who are young, but know God has a calling on your life; this is part of the process. God does not make mistakes. If you go through a storm, it is ordained by God. These types of storms are not meant to harm; they are meant to strengthen one's character.

Chapter Twenty-One

June 17, 2009

    I thank God once again for my life. Tomorrow, will be the seventh month since Wayne went to Heaven. I thank God for being a healer of broken hearts. I never thought I could feel such peace and contentment in my life. This serenity could not have been substituted by any man, woman, or child…only by God's mercy on me. I look back seven years ago exactly to this date: My divorce from Shawn was final. Look where He's brought me from! I was depressed, outraged, co-dependent, lost, insane…but God drove up in His Limo of mercy and told me, "Get in. I'm taking you somewhere far away from all this mess. I have plans for you and your girls, and when you get out of my Limo, you won't even remember the pain, just the ride." God kept His word. I can look at Shawn and smile, and I know in my heart I have no hard feelings. As a matter of fact, I can thank him because God used my divorce to save my soul. It's that "evil for your good" thing!!!

June 30, 2009

    Lord, I have yet another opportunity to say, "Thank you!" Thank you, for Loren and Ashley's Pell Grants. Thank you for Loren's getting into the dorm she wanted. Thank you for allowing me to have the *money to fix Loren's car. Thank you for allowing us to go on vacation for less than $500. Thank you for allowing Loren to get another job ten minutes after she was laid her off of her previous job! Lord, you have been so awesome to me! Even if you had not blessed me, you would still be awesome! But because you did bless me, I want to say, "You are awesome to me!"*

God has given me so much joy, and the joy of the Lord is surely my strength. Without the joy of the Lord, I wouldn't be able to wake up in the morning and smile and tell the Lord I love Him. Without His joy, I wouldn't be able to look at Wayne's picture without crying my eyes out! Without the joy of the Lord, I couldn't face my friends and family with a smile on my face and really mean it. I know what life is like without the joy of the Lord. I had experienced the great pain of loss. However, this time, God said this would be different. When Wayne died, I automatically assumed it would be like it had been when I lost Shawn, only ten times worse. I was ready for that familiar pain that I had known all throughout my late teen years up through my twenties as well as in my thirties. But up until now, I had never known the joy of the Lord. I have never been through this much fire and still lived to tell about it. I have always wanted to know what it was like to see the other side of a trial. I have always wanted to obtain all the blessings that God has laid up for me. Many times in church, I had heard different preachers speak of the blessings that He had in store for us, but the price was always too much for me to pay, and so I always got the bargain basement blessings. I was not willing to go to the next level up because it cost me more than I was willing to pay.

But this time around, the Devil took something that was worth more to me than pain and suffering. He really made me mad, and I told the Lord, "Whatever it takes for you to heal me, I will obey you. I will not use another relationship or any other distraction to dull my pain." I told God, "I will brace myself for the pain" and that I was ready for the fire! Then, I closed my eyes really tightly and waited for the freight train to run me over! But when I opened my eyes, God was the only one there. The pain was different, it was manageable, but at times it really did hurt. However, the difference was that I trusted God in the midst of my pain. I believed Him when I didn't even know what to believe Him for. The storm became even more intense against my heart and soul and mind. By the time the storm had passed over, I was so far from the coast that I couldn't retreat back to the familiar shore. I told the Lord in the Chapel at the hospital that no matter what He chose for Wayne, I would never be the same, and I would give Him my whole heart, mind, and body. So here I sit in a rowboat out in the middle of the Atlantic Ocean without oars, without a life jacket, a blanket, or any other form of shelter. Yet, I have peace; I have the covering of God's almighty hand. I have food and raiment. Where is my boat floating to? I don't know, but I do know Jesus is in the boat with me, and God is in control of my boat. Waves are all around me; sharks are swimming around the boat, too! It wouldn't be wise to get out of the boat. Jesus says, "Come to me, all who are weary and heavy-laden, and I will give you rest. (Matthew 11:28) And so I rest in the Lord. I don't worry about how I am going to pay my bills. My job is to simply trust God. Everyday, His mercies are new…Is my boat ever going to reach land? Will I be stuck out here in the middle of nowhere forever? What would make me ask that, besides the Devil? He is the only one who is in a boat going nowhere. That is why he is so mad. He uses our own thoughts to confuse us. God said, "I will never leave you or forsake you." I believe Him, and I trust Him. I know that God is taking me somewhere. I may not know where, but as I've acknowledged before," I trust Him." I know He would not hurt me nor trick me. God loves me!

July 13, 2009

I told the storm, "Pass, storm! You can't last!" Isn't it funny when we have a great testimony, the Devil hates it and tries to throw us off the mountain? Well, that was what happened to me. My unemployment was being held up. My first reaction was, "And here we go again!" but then I thought, "Yes, here we go again, and I am not going to worry myself sick about something that God is in control of." I put a relaxer in Mom's hair on Saturday, and she gave me fifty-five dollars. The next day was Seed Sunday at church; I didn't know it was Seed Sunday until I got there. I grabbed my money off the dresser and took it to service. I owed the Lord my tithe, which was thirty-five dollars, and so I had twenty left. The Lord said to me, "What can you do with twenty dollars?"

I said, "You're right, Lord; the question is, it's what you can do with twenty dollars," so I used it as a seed. That night Stephanie came by and left $160 in my accounting book! She said the Lord told her to give it to me. I have to pause and say, "What a mighty God we serve!"

July 13, 2009

I thank God for direction: On my morning's walk, God began to speak to me about the ministry He has planned for my life. I knew bits and pieces of what God wanted me to do, but I didn't fully know what, when, or where I would be doing these things. This morning, He made it clear to me. He said I would start at my home church EDF (New Bethel Tabernacle). He instructed me to have a meeting with Pastor Dee and talk about "Why Do You Cry Ministries." The first service would be a Singles Conference. God gave me specific instructions and whom I was to ask to speak along with me. God also told me to meet with Pastor Ramsey about Elder Dee's being covered by Pastor Ramsey as well as mentored by him. I have to talk to Pastor Dee about that, too. I am looking forward to what God has in store for WDYC Ministries. Lord, I want to thank you for not forgetting about this poor widow, who is now being transformed into a powerful woman of God. You're wonderful, beautiful, and glorious! Your name is matchless!

Chapter Twenty Two

August 3, 2009

Lord, I want to thank you for regulating my mind. As soon as God gave me that word, the Devil came in, but, like a flood, the Word of God washed over me! I almost didn't want to write. That is why there is such a large gap in the dates. Satan did everything he could to attack my mind. But I went to church Monday, and stood in that line because I wanted to be close to the front. I sat on the second row. Bishop Paul S. Morton was the speaker.

Let me tell you why this particular man of God is so special to me. Seven years earlier, I had met his nephew Jay. He became very good friends with the girls and me. At that time, I had never heard of Bishop Paul S. Morton, but as the years went by, I began to hear his name. When Wayne died, a CD was given to me called "I'm Still Standing" from Bishop Paul S. Morton's album. He talked about how he had lost his church and how he had gone through many difficult struggles in his life. I was also given a CD that had 15 worship songs on it. It was made by the Pastoral Care Team from New Life Worship Center. A man by the name, Minister Tommy gave it to me. Out of that whole album, two songs stood out, "Cry Your Last Tear" and "I Need Thee."

I would meditate on these two songs every day; I had no idea that Bishop Morton was the one who had recorded them. I just knew he had an awesome testimony, and I felt like God had given him a word for me, and he had!

Before the church service started, I met these two nice ladies. We stood in line together as we waited with anticipation for the doors of the church to open. These ladies just so happened to be in the Pastoral Care ministry. They asked me if I was interested in joining that ministry, and I said "yes," except I wasn't ready to go to any funerals just yet. One of the ladies remembered me because she was the one who had been trying to help me find Wayne's Bible. I didn't even remember her face, but she knew me. I shared with them my situation and why I was there to see the Bishop.

When we got in the sanctuary, we decided to sit together. Pastor Ramsey lifted the first offering and asked everyone to give a $20 seed. All I had was $5 bill that I had brought with me for offering, and one of the ladies saw me. She took a twenty dollar bill out of her wallet and gave it to me for offering. I gave her my five, but she would not accept it, so I thanked her and almost started crying. Bishop preached on waiting on God and not being afraid to step out on faith. The ladies kept looking at me. We laughed and "high-fived" all through the Word. At the end of Bishop's message, he asked for a $20 seed, and this same woman who had given me the first $20 seed reached in her purse and gave me another $20 seed! I cried as I hugged her. I told her she was a true example of love.

August 3, 2009 cont…

Thank you, Jesus! My Dad also sent me a text saying he had left me some money. When I got home, he had left me $500! So now I could pay my rent!

Earlier this week, I had had a meltdown because I thought that God was going to move like He did last month, but He was stretching my faith. I felt as if I was going to fall apart because I hated being late on my bills. God had different plans for me, and I was totally confused and upset that He hadn't come when I thought He should have. My faith was again stretched and shaken. I had to ask God for forgiveness for not trusting Him to do what was best for me. I am not out of the woods yet; I have to learn to trust God, even when it hurts to. I have had so many "no's" in the past 18 months, even before Wayne died. In my mind, I thought that I had suffered enough and that God would not stretch me any further than He already had. I felt like my mind could not take another delay from God. I was trying so hard not to get upset with God, but I let reasoning slip into my thoughts, and my emotions ran wild in my mind. I felt like I could not contain them.

Just the day before, Joyce Meyers had preached on letting your feelings get the best of you, and I heard the Word, but I let down my guard anyway. It was like the pressure was too great, and I couldn't hold it in anymore. I cried all day Friday, Saturday, and part of Sunday. I thank God for sending the Word Sunday morning and night and again through the Bishop on Monday.

Today is a better day, not because things have changed, but because God's mercies are new every day. Today is another opportunity to trust God and to wait on His promises of deliverance. Ashley wrote on my board in my room, "When you're down to nothing, God is up *to something." The day is going to come when I will be the person slipping $20 bills in my neighbors' hands and smiling at them.*

August 4, 2009

"I will bless the Lord at all times, and His praises shall continually be in my mouth." Today was an interesting day. I could hear God teaching me His ways all morning. The Lord gave me a message: "The Lady and the Weed Whacker." I chuckle at the analogies that God gives me. They are so funny, yet so true. We really have to be in a receiving mode for God to be able to teach us. God normally teaches me things when I am frustrated by something that I need to do, but the equipment isn't working properly. I have had a lot of life lessons, working at Chrysler.

This morning, I had purposed in my heart that I would clean up my yard. It didn't have trash; it just needed to be cut and trimmed. I noticed that it needed to be trimmed more than mowed, and so I got the weed whacker out of the garage and proceeded to trim. The weed eater line kept breaking, and I had to keep taking it apart every five minutes. I must have fixed it seven times in a 40-minute period. Every time I would cut near something that had a little resistance such as the cement stairs, the line would break. As I sat down to fix the weed eater for the eighth time or so, I noticed that I wasn't getting upset. It was as though I had peace about what I was doing, which was unusual because it was now 12 o'clock noon and it was hot outside. I began to hear the Lord say to me, "If you can figure out how to run this machine correctly, then it will work properly for you."

I just said in my spirit, "Yes, Lord, that is true." My thoughts went back to my husband and how he used to use the Same equipment. I laughed at myself as a funny thought entered into my mind: "This is the number one reason why women want to get married, to get out of yard work."

I then heard the Lord say, "It's just an excuse. You can do all things through Christ."

I replied, "That is true, Lord." I thought about how my husband would tap on the ground and the string would advance itself so he wouldn't have to keep taking it apart. That worked until I ran out of string. I had bought some more string, so I went to the garage to retrieve the string, and I noticed it was a little heavier than the other string that had been previously on there. At first, I didn't think I could replace the string because I had never done that before. It was a little confusing because the hole where the string fit was too small for the larger string. I noticed that there was another hole on the opposite side, and I got great satisfaction from finding that little discrepancy. As I wound the thicker string around the device, I noticed that it kept unraveling, and I kept trying. Finally, after 15 minutes of maneuvering the string, I got the weed eater ready to go again.

I began using it, and the thought (the Lord) came to me to listen for a certain sound, and I did. I could tell the difference when the string was breaking and when I needed to tap it on the ground to advance the string. I thought about the process that it took to take the weed eater apart and to fix the string and put it back together. The Lord began to speak to me and tell me it was necessary that I go through the process of the string breaking and the practice of taking the machine apart and putting it back together. Every time I had to repeat the process, I got faster and better at it. "Now you are learning to listen so that you do not have to repeat the process of taking the machine apart. The new string you put on there is stronger. If you had not broken the other string off, you would have never gotten to the place where you could have a stronger piece of string. Even though the weaker string kept breaking and you kept fixing it , you didn't give up. Now that you have the new string on there, it is stronger and it won't break as easily. If you listen to the machine, you can hear the different sounds as the string gets shorter and when you tap, you can hear the string advancing."

I listened carefully and continued to trim faster than I had all morning. The string never broke again from that moment on. I was able to go back and trim the weeds that the weaker string could not cut. The strong string cut right through them. I thought, "That is how life is when we fail at the simple trials of life. God replaces us with a stronger string so that we can go back and cut through the trials that used to break us down." Then I wondered if anyone had seen me out there struggling and if that person had thought, "This Lady is not going to give up!" And I wasn't! My mind was made up that I was going to finish what I had started, and I could hear God cheering me on. About five minutes later, a car pulled up to me, and my neighbor said, "You can trim mine when you're done." I laughed to myself and thought that there was always someone watching whether we realized it or not. Another thought came to me as I wiped my sweaty brow: It really wasn't that hot outside. It was only 78 degrees, but it felt like a hundred. God brought to my mind this: No matter how cool it is around us, it will always seem hot if we are working. If the people around us aren't feeling some kind of heat, we need to ask them, "Are you working?"

Chapter Twenty Three

August 21, 2009

Lord, I first give you honor and praise. I'm sitting some place where I thought I wouldn't be for a while, in the hospital. I'm at the bedside of a friend who is in the hospital, fighting cancer. I never thought I would be back here with yet another man that I cared about, watching him fight for his life. He called me yesterday and told me he was in the hospital and asked me if I would come and see him. I felt apprehensive about going to see him because of our past.

When I walked in, Craig looked better than I thought he would look. He still looked healthy, even though I knew he was very sick. I talked to my family members about going to see him. They asked me if I was willing to get involved with someone else that was sick after going through such an ordeal of pain with Wayne. I guess I didn't think of it in the same way. Wayne was my husband; I didn't have a choice. Everything had happened so suddenly. I would have walked through fire with Wayne, and I did. But Craig had a progressive sickness, plus we were not dating. I was just visiting him at the hospital. I always believed that God was going to heal him. The same faith I had had for Wayne was the same faith that I had for Craig when I walked into the hospital. I didn't allow the doubt and fear of cancer to change my mind.

When I walked in the hospital, there was a familiar sense of dread. For some reason, walking into Community East Hospital didn't bother me, but St. Vincent was where Wayne had died, not that particular St. Vincent but it felt all the same to me. I walked into the large hospital, and it seemed as though it would take me forever to get to his room. When I finally walked into Craig's room, I said hello and his face lit up like the Fourth of July. He asked me for a hug, and I leaned in to give him one. As I was hugging him, he whispered in my ear, "I still love you, Lori."

I rose up and asked, "What did you say?" and he repeated what he had said.

I sat down, and he began to apologize for the past. He told me he was sorry for hurting me, for not believing me, as well as for the way he had treated me. He told me God had dealt with his pride along with his being a player. He said he wanted a wife to love and to take care of and that he just wanted to put away the petty fighting and enjoy his life. He told me God was calling him to ministry. I always knew that. I just couldn't understand why he had acted like he was crazy.

When I got to my car, I just sat there and stared out the window. I gathered my thoughts and began to pray and ask God what to do. I thanked Him, too, because God answered a prayer that I had prayed about four years ago...for God to save Craig, and just like me, this was what it took for Craig to be saved.

August 22, 2009

This was day number two; I promised Craig I would come back up to the hospital to see him. The doctors were going to put him in isolation for a week or so, and so I decided to visit one more time before they did. We talked most of the evening, and I shared the part of my book about when we first met; I also read through our dating, the proposal, and all the madness of the infamous car chase through Carmel, IN. We laughed so hard at the stupidity of our fights and all the drama that followed. He agreed that I was accurate. I made sure of it because I did not want him to be caught off guard. It was important to me that he knew he was a big part of my book. I never thought in a million years that I would be talking and laughing with him about such a difficult part of my life. I had thought I would never be completely healed from all the drama of 2005, but God is the God of restoration and healing.

August 27, 2009

Dear Jesus, I cannot even begin to thank you for your intersession in my life. I thank you for blessing me with a job. Monday was my first day. I went to orientation, which was long and boring, but I was excited about starting my new job. Tuesday, while at lunch, I got a phone call from my union steward, at Chrysler. He asked me if I was willing to accept $75,000 plus a $25,000 car voucher as a severance package from Chrysler. I could not believe this was happening! God was fulfilling His promises to me! I told the union steward, "Yes, I accept." I could not wait to get off work to go to Kokomo and sign the papers.

Words cannot express my joy! However, that was not all that happened; God had also blessed me with even more money, close to $5,000 all in the same week. The Lord had promised He was coming to see about me. I just could not imagine that it would be so overwhelming and so sudden. It was as if one day, I was grateful for my rent being paid (I couldn't care less if I had a dollar left over as long as my bills were paid), and the next, there was an abundance of rain…more than enough, an overflow plus a brand new car that was paid in full…no more car note! I had had less than $5,000 in bills, and now I was debt free! God, you are awesome!

I don't know what my future holds, but I definitely know who holds my future. God gave me **an expected end**. What the Devil meant for my evil, God meant for my good. This is the first time I have ever seen the end of a trial and actually made it to the other side. I know God is not done with me yet; He is just getting started. It has been a seven-year journey to bring me to this place of rest, peace, and joy.

I imagine that you are probably wondering what happened with Craig and me? Well, at this time we are just friends. We are both seeking God for our own direction…Craig, for his, as a man who is destined to carry God's word; and I, for mine, as a woman who is destined to go God's way and do the same thing. The Bible says if our ways are pleasing unto the Lord, He will give us the desires of our heart. My desire is to please God. I cannot live without Him; everything and everyone else are secondary to Christ.

Whatever happened to Shawn, the ex-husband? God totally healed my heart of the divorce. It no longer matters that he didn't express regret for his part: Forgiveness has to be unconditional. Don't get me wrong: It took me seven years to accomplish all of this because I was so stubborn to the idea of submitting completely to God. Today, Shawn and his wife Alva are very good friends with me. They have a precious baby boy who just turned one year old. No kidding, Alva and I are really friends! I love her. It's nothing but God. He deserves all the glory!

I do want every person who is reading this to understand that God wants us to seek after Him with all of our heart. The transition takes time. There are no five-minute miracles when it comes to God transforming our lives. I do not think I truly understood that until I had nothing left to give God, but my heart. It was shattered, and I knew that no one could fix it but Jesus. Believe me, I tried to find someone else. If it were not for the trials that God allowed in my life, I would not be saved today. The reason for storms is to save us, as well as bring us into a deeper relationship with the Father. There is purpose for our pain; we must go through the storms of life to find out what that purpose is. After the storm, there is also a reward for our pain and suffering. serenity comes immediately after we surrender to God's will for our life. It does not mean that God will give us our way; it means that peace will come quickly.

There is no amount of money that can replace the peace that God freely gave me during the most painful moments of my life. God covered me and hid me in His arms. He held me every time I cried, and sometimes it hurt so badly that I wanted to die, but He wouldn't let me give up. This is why I serve Him every day.

I am now in love with a man named Jesus. He has won me over, not with money or a mate, but with His ability to bring me to a point of awareness that He truly loved me first. I now understand why I had to cry, and it is now time for you to discover the answer to the same question: **"Why Do You Cry?"**

"Those who sow in tears, shall reap in joy!" (Psalms 126:5)

November 24, 2009

This book is dedicated to my late husband Wayne Gerard Edwards. Thank you for pushing me to finish writing this book. Thank you for encouraging me when I thought this was just a pipe dream. Your love inspired me to continue to write even when my heart was hurting, and I was missing you. As I come to the end of this journey, and proof reading this book for the fifth time, my eyes are full of tears and joy! I can't wait to see where God is going to take me next.

Lori L. Edwards